GETTING TENURE

D0870577

SURVIVAL SKILLS FOR SCHOLARS

Managing Editor: Mitchell Allen

Survival Skills for Scholars provides you, the professor or advanced graduate student working in a college or university setting, with practical suggestions for making the most of your academic career. These brief, readable guides will help you with skills that you are required to master as a college professor but may have never been taught in graduate school. Using hands-on, jargon-free advice and examples, forms, lists, and suggestions for additional resources, experts on different aspects of academic life give invaluable tips on managing the day-to-day tasks of academia—effectively and efficiently.

Volumes in This Series

SURVIVAL SKILLS FOR SCHOLARS

GETTING TENURE

MARCIA LYNN WHICKER

JENNIE JACOBS KRONENFELD

RUTH ANN STRICKLAND

SAGE Publications
International Educational and Professional Publisher
Newbury Park   London   New Delhi

Copyright © 1993 by Sage Publications, Inc.

For information address:

 SAGE Publications, Inc.
2455 Teller Road
Newbury Park, California 91320

SAGE Publications Ltd.
6 Bonhill Street
London EC2A 4PU
United Kingdom

SAGE Publications India Pvt. Ltd.
M-32 Market
Greater Kailash I
New Delhi 110 048 India

Printed in the United States of America

Library of Congress Cataloging-in-Publication Data

Getting tenure / Marcia Lynn Whicker, Jennie Jacobs
    Kronenfeld, Ruth Ann Strickland.
        p.   cm.   —   (Survival skills for scholars ; vol. 8)
    Includes bibliographical references (p.).
    ISBN 0-8039-5302-X — ISBN 0-8039-5303-8 (pbk.)
    1. College teachers—Tenure—United States. I. Whicker, Marcia
Lynn. II. Kronenfeld, Jennie J. III. Strickland, Ruth Ann.
IV. Series.
LB2335.7.G48   1993
378.1'22—dc20   93-20711
                                                                         CIP

93 94 95 96 10 9 8 7 6 5 4 3 2 1

Sage Production Editor: Megan M. McCue

Contents

1 | Thinking About Tenure

Tenure is a powerful force. A desire for tenure at times grips people as strongly as a desire for romantic love. The outcome of both tenure and love shape and mold one's self-image and self-esteem. Success is cause for great joy and celebration. Failure implies dejection and defeat. The prospect of earning tenure, like love, provides a roller coaster of emotions. As prospects brighten, emotions soar. As prospects dampen, gloom and doom set in. At times, both tenure and love force people to pursue activities past the point of fatigue. Both tenure and love make some people sensitive to others. Both make some people crazy. Consider the following contrast.

John was at a medium-sized state university. As a junior professor, he wanted tenure. John taught Marxism and socialist thought in a political science department before the Cold War ended. He knew that others perceived the philosophy he taught as ill-founded and dangerous. Although John personally was neither a Marxist nor a socialist, he had leftist leanings. This was not unusual, because faculty members often tend to study and specialize in things they personally find fascinating. John lived in a conservative state. Some older colleagues in his department had poked fun at John's leftist leanings at department lunches. Rather than respond angrily, John took the ribbing in good nature and would crack a joke at conservative philosophy in return.

John took tenure seriously. He had a wife and small child to support. His wife wanted more children. They liked their current home and wanted to stay. This meant John must get tenure. John spent many long evenings working on articles and papers that he submitted to journals. Typically they were rejected on the first round but usually accepted for publication after several revisions at the second or third journal to which he submitted them. His publications grew at an acceptable if not fast rate.

John was also conscientious about teaching. At his large state university, many students, especially the "frat boys" and "sorority gals" were suspicious of him initially. Sometimes these suspicious students were forced to take John for a required course. His earnestness at explaining the material, coupled with his concern that all students feel free to discuss issues, provoked interesting discussions. Soon the students realized that they could speak up even if they did not agree with John or the class material. Heated debates between students with leftist and more conservative perspectives would ensue. Rarely did less serious or conservative students take John's elective courses, so those classes did not have the lively exchanges that typified his required courses. But John won the respect if not the enthusiasm of a wide range of students.

One day at John's university, the cafeteria and maintenance workers went on strike. Most workers made minimum wage or slightly above. They protested that they could not feed their families and wanted a larger raise. The workers contended that the state had allocated money for their raises to the university administration, which was spending it for other purposes. The workers also contended that the percentage raise they wanted was no bigger than what higher-level administrators were receiving. The union for the workers beseeched the faculty to join them in protest marches, and failing that, to at least not cross the picket line.

Several faculty members in John's department, including powerful tenured members, decided to ignore the strike. John agonized that he would be labeled as a "leftist kook" if he supported the workers. He worried that his classes would suffer if they did not meet and that his students would not cover the required material. But, he also thought, how better to illustrate the points made in the readings than the worker strike unfolding before them on their own campus. John seized the opportunity. To support the workers, he did not cross the picket line to hold class, although he arranged for his classes to meet in a nearby recreation hall. He invited the leaders of the strike as well as a member of the university administration to his classes to discuss the issues involved in the strike. He wrote a piece for the local newspaper expounding the two views, the points of difference, and the points of common interest. It was read throughout the community. One local television station called John to provide an expert opinion. John was so skilled at analyzing the issues, his colleagues now cracked that perhaps he had a future as a labor negotiator or conflict mediator. After two weeks the strike ended. John then wrote an academic article from his experiences, discussing the philosophical, moral, and economic issues involved in labor issues at state universities. This article was published and increased John's peer-reviewed articles for tenure.

When John's tenure decision came up a year and a half later, even the senior colleagues who had cracked about John being a leftist noted how balanced he had been in a volatile and potentially disruptive situation. They commented on how he had not violated his own views but had personal integrity and found a compromise solution during the strike. Because John had been working hard and had been reasonably productive, he had an adequate number of articles and acceptable teaching evaluations. His work with media as well as campus and department activities allowed him to have enough service. John received a strong tenure-approval vote in his department. The dissenters were two older faculty members who had never liked him. The night his tenure was finalized, his wife threw a dinner party for some close friends. They all celebrated with good food and fine wine. John exuded a warm glow the whole evening.

At the same state university, Joe arrived on campus as a young untenured assistant professor the same year as John. Joe was hired in the philosophy department. Joe also wanted tenure. His wife, Mary, was a poet and artist who worked with a local craft store and taught art classes occasionally. She also wrote and had published one volume. Both Joe and Mary wore faded blue jeans everywhere with torn-out knees and patches. They were always present at the premieres of new foreign and art films at the local Bijou Theater.

Joe quickly became a very popular teacher, making old dead "masters" come to life. Joe began to act like a buddy to the students, which also boosted his popularity. He would show up at the local student pub and drink pitchers of beers with some of the students. Occasionally Mary joined him at first, but eventually she stopped. Originally Joe would do this only at Friday afternoon happy hours, but after two or three years, he could be seen at the student pub several nights a week. Joe was good-looking and there always seemed to be a cluster of attractive female students as well as male students around him.

Joe kept an open-door policy at the office and was always willing to talk to students. Sometimes he would show up at faculty meetings late because a student had come by with a problem and, being sensitive and supportive, he was unwilling to cut off the conversation prematurely to go to a department meeting. Joe tried initially to publish articles from his dissertation, working mostly at his office. He did send two articles out. One was rejected at the first journal but eventually accepted at a second journal. The second got a "revise and resubmit" notice from the editor, but Joe never got around to revising it. When so many students started coming by, Joe found it impossible to do serious intellectual work at his office. He intended to go home after class and work, but more often he stopped at the student pub.

Joe's concern with students and his ability to talk to them on their own terms and in their own language won him two teaching awards. One was offered by a philosophy student association on campus. The second was quite prestigious and was a campuswide teaching award. These made Joe feel very good: He truly was gifted in his work. He felt that he mattered to the students and made a difference in their lives. When Joe's tenure decision came up, however, he did not get a positive department vote. The big book he was working on was still half-done, and Joe did not have that many articles published. His teaching evaluations were excellent and his classes were huge successes, but some older professors were suspicious of his methods. A couple even muttered that he "pandered" to the students. No one commented directly on his drinking at the student pub. Because other faculty members did not hang out at the student pub, many may not have been aware of Joe's many hours there. Some colleagues commented, however, that he did not maintain the proper distance with students.

Joe had been a little nervous preparing his tenure file, but he was running on manic energy in a state of denial about the likelihood of him being rejected. He thought the university would not dare to fire such a popular teacher who had won a campuswide teaching award. When his department chair told him his case did not get a positive department vote, Joe became hostile in the meeting. He accused his colleagues of being jealous of his teaching success and his popularity with students. The department chair told Joe he could finish out this year teaching, plus he would have one more year on a terminal contract to find another job.

Joe decided to appeal his tenure denial. He implored his favorite students to write letters and sign petitions on his behalf. They complied. Many department colleagues saw this as inappropriately involving students in a university personnel matter. Joe became alienated from his colleagues. His case continued forward under appeal, but no one at any level overturned the negative outcome. The next year, Joe sent out several job applications to other colleges and universities. No university similar to the one where he was working was interested.

During his terminal year at the university, Joe had one interview at a small, religiously based college 200 miles away.

From the minute he set foot on that campus, where students wore neatly tailored, pressed, and conservative clothes and the professors looked like cookie cutter ads for Brooks Brothers, Joe felt it to be a mistake. Although Joe did wear a faded and torn tweed jacket with a bold flowery tie and a pink shirt to the interview, he insisted on also wearing his standard faded blue jeans. He made a concession by selecting a pair without torn knees. During the interview, he made little effort to conceal how uptight he found the college to be. Needless to say, he did not get the job.

Back at his university, Joe made one big last-ditch effort to get the students to petition the university president, often called "Big Jim" on campus, to overturn his denial in the spring of his terminal year. The effort failed, and Big Jim let normal university processes fire Joe without personally intervening. That spring Mary left Joe. When classes ended, he had nowhere to go and nothing to do. He had not run out of money yet, but he was now seen drinking in the student pub and other bars for long hours.

Joe floated in and out of town for a year or more after that. Slowly, the students who knew him and who used to clap enthusiastically at the end of his lectures graduated and moved on with their lives, even as Joe was having a hard time moving on in his. Fewer and fewer of them remembered Joe. Sometimes those who had not known him before were stunned when older students told them that Joe used to be a professor. By now, he looked more seedy than professorial. With just a few drinks, he was more likely to launch into an angry diatribe than an erudite dialectic.

Sometimes Joe would say he was working for a distributor out of Florida. Sometimes he said he was on the payroll of an unidentified family business. At times he even implied he was working for the CIA! His stories were so varied and contradictory, the few remaining friends he had eventually just quit asking what he was doing or where he was working. Having once pondered the meaning of life's deepest questions, Joe was now reduced to pondering who was the best pool player, which ball would go into the pocket, and how fast cigarette ashes would fall. Joe continued to come and go for weeks at a time. Finally, he just went. No one was sure where he had gone. He just stopped coming to town. He never reappeared in the profession again.

The tenure cases of both John and Joe occurred at about the same time in the same place. One had a happy ending, the other a tragic ending. Fortunately, most tenure denials do not end in death. But the denial of tenure can be emotionally devastating. Some people take years to recover the self-esteem they lose from tenure denial. Other people never fully recover and remain bitter and scarred.

Fortunately, too, almost all happy tenure outcomes are celebrated with good friends, good food, and joy. We hope you are among this joyful contingent. Just as with the cases of John and Joe, your tenure decision is not preordained. Like John, there are things you can do to help your tenure prospects. Like Joe, there are things you should avoid that will hurt those prospects. If you want to join John among the tenured professoriate, we wrote this book for you. In it we will explore why tenure exists, what it means, how people get it, and strategies and pressures surrounding tenure decisions and processes.

How do we know about these questions? Each of us has endured various aspects of the tenure process and know personally the trauma, fears, and rewards it holds. Marcia first received tenure at a large state university and has since moved twice, going through external tenure processes at each subsequent location. Jennie was granted tenure early in her fourth year of teaching and also has subsequently moved on to receive tenure at two other universities. Ruth Ann has been promoted early and is in the throes of the tenure process as we write.

Both Marcia and Jennie have served on department, schoolwide, and universitywide tenure committees at different universities. Counting our graduate school universities, collectively we have personally observed tenure decisions at different levels at 10 different universities! Our combined teaching experience is 41 years. Marcia has worked in political science and public administration; Jennie in sociology and public health, including appointments in a medical school and a business school; and Ruth Ann in political science and criminal justice. We have been in universities in most parts of the country: Marcia in the Border South, Midwest, South, and Northeast; Jennie in the Northeast, South, and West; and Ruth Ann in the South. During this time we have developed networks around the country in various fields, expanding our observations across disciplines.

We aim to give you practical knowledge about how to prepare for your tenure decision. As you will see, there is no single path to tenure. But, just as when all roads used to lead to Rome, in modern universities and colleges all roads lead to a tenure decision for those who wish to make academia their place of work. We wish you well in your endeavors. If you are reading this book, you are already thinking about things you must do to clear that hurdle. Here's to your safe landing on the other side!

What Is Tenure?

Tenure has different meanings to you and your university or college. The basic meaning of tenure to you is job security. But tenure is also a merit reward for a job well done as well as a career motivator. To your college, tenure is a protection of academic freedom, a multimillion dollar institutional investment, and a legislative personnel process. (See Figure 1.1.) Let us briefly explore these various meanings as well as the regulation of tenure before turning to specific strategies for getting tenure and stages in the tenure process.

Job Security

Tenure is job security. Tenure means you cannot be fired for trivial reasons. If you get a new department chair who does

To you, tenure is:

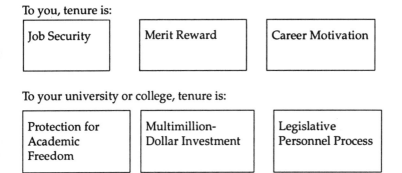

| Job Security | Merit Reward | Career Motivation |

To your university or college, tenure is:

| Protection for Academic Freedom | Multimillion-Dollar Investment | Legislative Personnel Process |

Figure 1.1. What Is Tenure?

not like you, that chair has little or no recourse to try to get rid of you if you have tenure. Tenure also means that you are not at the mercy or whims of deans, provosts, presidents, or department chairs. Tenure is a powerful protection, indeed! Tenured professors have among the "safest" jobs in the world. They can stand up to those in higher administration without fearing job loss and major financial repercussions.

A Merit Reward

Tenure is a merit reward for a job well done. Faculty are expected to perform in three areas: (a) scholarship and research, (b) teaching, and (c) service. Tenure is the reward for meeting performance expectations in these three main areas. In some colleges, two additional, more minor criteria are used in the tenure decision: (d) professional training and educational credentials and (e) collegiality. (See Table 1.1.)

Most colleges formally state that the three criteria are weighted equally. Informal norms, however, as well as the track records of successful candidates from the past may indicate otherwise. Universities often informally weight scholarship and research as the most important criterion of the three for getting tenure.

Table 1.1 Criteria for Tenure

Standard criteria:
1. Scholarship and research.
   Evidence: Peer-reviewed publications
                Books
                Scholarly presentations
                Positive reviews of publications
                Citations of publications and other evidence of impact
                Grants for research
2. Teaching.
   Evidence: Student-teaching evaluations
                Peer observations of classroom teaching
                Letters from former students
                Success of graduate students
                Teaching awards
3. Service.
   Evidence: Professional association offices and committees
                Editorial boards of journals
                Review activities for journals
                University committee service
                Department committee service
                Statistical, methodological, or computer assistance for
                   colleagues
                Community talks and technical assistance
                Faculty adviser to student associations

Less common but occasionally used criteria:
4. Professional training and credentials.
   Evidence: Specialized credentials such as medical specialties,
                   board certifications, and professional licenses
5. Collegiality.
   Evidence: Supportive letters from department colleagues and
                   other faculty members

Scholarship and Research

The so-called publish-or-perish shibboleth evolved at major universities. In such settings, inadequate teaching may create difficulties in receiving a positive tenure recommendation, although a superb publishing record may compensate for weak or mediocre teaching. Stellar teaching, however, rarely is sufficient to compensate for a weak or inadequate publishing record. Traditionally, the higher the prestige of the university, the greater the emphasis placed on research and scholarship, and the less the emphasis on teaching and service. Peer-reviewed publications count more than the nonpeer-reviewed. In some fields, getting research grants is an important part of meeting the scholarship criterion. Other evidence of research productivity includes books, scholarly presentations, positive reviews of publications, and other evidence of research impact. This criterion is addressed more fully in Chapter 5.

Teaching

In contrast to the greater emphasis placed on research and scholarship at large universities, small liberal arts colleges often place more emphasis on the teaching criterion. Such colleges may have small departments in any particular field. Faculty in small departments may be called on to teach a wide array of courses so that students get repeated exposure to the same faculty member as they take courses in their major. In such a setting, the college can ill afford to tolerate weak or even mediocre teaching. Teaching here is more important than research. Teaching performance is judged by student evaluations as well as peer review by fellow faculty members observing the classroom performance of tenure candidates. Supportive letters from former students and teaching awards are also evidence of superior teaching. Chapter 6 discusses strategies to meet the teaching criterion.

Service

Neither large universities nor small liberal arts colleges usually place primary emphasis on the service criterion, but it is not unimportant. Service in a university setting may require national and international exposure in the academic discipline through participation on journal editorial boards and peer review panels for grants. Committee work and holding office in disciplinary professional associations also gains national visibility. Service in a small liberal arts college may focus more on student- and campus-related activities. Campus service includes serving as an advisor to student associations and discipline-related clubs, as well as facilitating student trips and other learning activities. Liberal arts college service also may focus on service on important campus committees such as fund raising, upgrading computer skills, and developing curricula. Chapter 7 examines strategies for meeting the service criterion.

Professional Training and Credentials

Not all colleges and universities use the additional criteria of professional credentials and collegiality, but some do. Adequate professional credentials are usually necessary to get a tenure-track job and therefore are not an issue at tenure time. The relevant terminal degree, typically a Ph.D. from an accredited university, usually is considered proof of adequate training. Regional accrediting bodies for colleges require schools to maintain a high proportion of faculty members who hold terminal degrees. Fields in which degrees other than the Ph.D. may be accepted as the terminal degree include some performing arts (Master's in Fine Arts, or M.F.A.), law (Doctorate of Jurisprudence, or J.D.), and medicine (Doctorate of Medicine, or M.D.). On rare occasions, the standard of holding the terminal degree may be violated. In the field of creative writing, for example, other prizes and publications may be accepted in lieu of the terminal degree in granting tenure to well-known authors. Such cases constitute infrequent exceptions, however, rather than the norm.

Although the terminal degree may be the only proof of adequate professional credentials needed in most fields, other credentials may be desirable in specialized fields. Accountants who have passed the Certified Public Accountant (C.P.A.)

exam may use that credential as further proof of their fitness for tenure. Tenure candidates in medicine may submit specialized residencies and certificates as proof of relevant professional training. Law professors who have passed appropriate bar examinations and who hold specialized degrees beyond the J.D. may also submit those credentials as part of their tenure justification.

Collegiality

An occasionally used fifth criterion of "collegiality" is controversial. It may be used to weed out candidates who do not "fit" or who are not good department citizens. Before tenure, you will be able to get away with alienating one or even two powerful department members who already hold tenure, depending on the size of the department. But alienating most of the tenured members is almost always fatal.

Tenured members view your tenure decision as selecting you as a long-term, if not a lifetime, colleague. If they feel anxious, nervous, threatened, irritated, or angry with you at work, you probably will be rejected. Tenure criteria are sufficiently vague, and the standards applied to each criteria are sufficiently evolving in most institutions that grounds for rejecting all but the most brilliant candidates can be found. You plainly do not want to be perceived as unpleasant, venal, unethical, or unprofessional by current department and institutional standards. Although you do not want to pretend to be someone you are not, idiosyncracies and eccentricities that may be interpreted as disagreeable rather than charming are better downplayed until after tenure.

A Career Motivator

Tenure is a career motivator. Before tenure you may feel pressure to participate in research projects and service activities only tangential to your primary interests for the sake of building a tenurable record. Few opportunities can be turned down, especially those that hold the promise of creating another "line on the vita." Yet chasing after opportunities with rapid payoff can be mentally and physically exhausting. By contrast, you may feel liberated after receiving tenure and free to pursue broader, long-range, and riskier research questions. True, after receiving tenure, some faculty members subsequently sink into lethargy and vegetate. But also common is the opposite: the energizing and increased focus of those who make it through the process. The benefits include greater psychological satisfaction and enhanced prospects of breakthrough discoveries for the academic discipline and for society. Intellectual breakthroughs and paradigm shifts are frequently preceded by failed trial runs. Tenured faculty have the luxury of trying research avenues that do not pan out; untenured faculty do not.

Protection of Academic Freedom

The formal rationale for tenure is protection of academic freedom. Proponents of tenure argue that professors who are curbed by any authority—the federal government, state government, university administrators, board of trustees members, or even students or an outraged public—lack the freedom needed to explore new ideas and theories unimpeded. New scientific ideas and theories are often controversial and unpopular before they are proven, and sometimes even afterwards. In the humanities and arts, new perspectives are not "proven" in a scientific sense and may also stimulate controversy as well as valuable insight into the human condition. Professors who must worry about political whims and popular ignorance lack the academic freedom needed to do groundbreaking scholarship or even, in disputed areas, journeyman technical research. Tenure overcomes this roadblock to intellectual progress by granting not only job security for keepers of the social knowledge base, but also great autonomy in how those jobs are executed.

Proponents of the tenure system point to periods where mass hysteria may have driven out of universities scholars who held unpopular views. During the McCarthy era of the 1950s, for example, communistic leanings were unpopular and sanctioned in most institutions within society. Prominent film and television stars and journalists who had the slightest trace of communist sympathies in their background were blackballed and prevented from working. But left-leaning professors with tenure could not be fired. Tenure protected professors who held unpopular views.

In the 1960s, protest against the Vietnam War grew slowly. Universities became major crucibles for developing antiwar arguments and protests. Without tenure, professors protesting the war could have been fired. Likewise, professors who examine any cause unpopular at the time—from civil rights for blacks to the feminist movement, to gay rights—can do so without fear of job reprisals if they have earned tenure.

Tenure, then, is supposed to allow the free exchange of ideas, which it often does. Tenure is important in all settings, but especially in state universities and colleges that are ultimately controlled by state legislators and governors and their appointed boards of trustees. These politicians are under pressure from the public and sometimes self-imposed pressure to make universities eschew unpopular causes. But tenure ensures that their ability to force professors to study and advocate only politically popular causes will be muted. When tenure works to achieve this end, it is a good thing! It ensures academic freedom and promotes the growth of knowledge, unimpeded by a cumbersome political ideology.

A Multimillion-Dollar Institutional Investment

Although you are preoccupied with the development of a personal tenurable academic record before the tenure clock expires, college administrators view your tenure as a multiyear, multimillion-dollar institutional investment. If you pursue academics as a first career, your tenure decision occurs at a relatively young age. An undergraduate who goes straight through undergraduate school will normally earn a college degree by age 22.

A fast-tracking 22-year-old graduate going straight into graduate school may earn his or her Ph.D. in three or four years, a very short but plausible time in which to complete a doctorate. More typically, a Ph.D. student takes 5 to 7 years to complete doctoral training. Even so, the typical Ph.D. graduate who went straight through undergraduate and graduate school without a significant break is younger than 30.

If you land a tenure track job before age 30, you could be reviewed for tenure before the age of 35. Tenure reviews of faculty in their early 30s are not uncommon, and precocious faculty may be reviewed at an even younger age. The college granting you tenure is guaranteeing you lifetime employment subject to dismissal only on very limited grounds. If you work to age 70, your tenure represents a salary and fringe-benefits commitment of another 35 years.

Not all tenure cases are clearly positive or negative decisions beforehand. Although professional colleagues who work daily with a likable tenure candidate may choose in ambiguous cases to err on the side of granting tenure, college administrators concerned about the ability to meet future financial obligations may choose to err on the side of denying tenure, given its long-term commitment. University administrators, more than colleagues, are likely to recognize the severe mistake of "tenuring in deadwood." Both administrators and faculty members may see the costs of tenuring any specific candidate: Someone tenured today means one less person to tenure in the next few years. The more prestigious the university or college, the greater the likelihood that current tenure candidates will have to compete indirectly not only with other current tenure candidates, but also against perceptions of university administrators of how good future tenure candidates are likely to be.

A Legislative Personnel Process

Tenure may also be viewed as a legislative process. Administrators recognize the impact that peer decisions have on tenure outcomes. If you also acknowledge this aspect of tenure, then you are in a better position to manage the process and to position yourself favorably. This view of tenure will be addressed in greater detail in Chapter 2.

The AAUP Regulation of Tenure

The American Association of University Professors (AAUP) is a labor union for faculty members. It has published rules about the tenure process that normally guide how tenure is granted in various universities. Even universities and colleges without an active AAUP bargaining unit usually adhere to AAUP tenure rules, which cover several aspects of tenure.

Tenure is normally granted at the department level. This means that tenure is received in a particular unit or department. Your job security is attached to the fate of that particular academic department, although most universities try to honor tenure across departments by finding positions for tenured faculty in other departments or units if one unit is abolished.

AAUP rules specify that you have six years to earn tenure. In most settings, if you are in a tenure-granting position and the university does not review you formally for tenure, merely continuing to employ you beyond the tenure decision point is equivalent to granting tenure. Some few people have even gotten tenure by oversight! Given the scarcity of tenure positions, however, such mistakes rarely occur today—and you certainly should not count on it.

Once tenured, you are usually a full member of the university community and are eligible to participate in the tenure decisions of others. In one sense, tenure decisions are somewhat similar to a fraternity rush party in which existing club members pick the new members. Of course, the criteria for selecting members of the academic "fraternity" are very different from those used by student social fraternities. It is important to pay attention to the tenure criteria at your school. John did. Joe did not. And therein lay their fates.

2 | Managing Your Tenure Case

The prospect of earning tenure need not be overwhelming. Just remember that you are already doing what it takes to earn tenure in most places: being a good academic and doing your job as a professor. But also remember that *attaining tenure is political*, like most processes in complex organizations. If you do not understand the political nature of tenure, your ignorance can hurt you. But the fact that politics is an important part of the tenure process does not necessarily have to work against you. Once you understand this, you can make the political character of tenure work for you. Much like a floor manager in a legislature maneuvering his bill through legislative committees and hurdles, you can manage your own tenure case.

University administrators have already been trained to think of tenure as a political, legislative personnel process operating under peer decisions. Thinking this way may help you as well put your best foot forward before and during your tenure decision. Your political skill is not the only determinant of your tenure case outcome or even in some instances the most important one. But you cannot afford to take politics for granted. Manage your own tenure case. Devise strategies to use the political aspects of the process and become a good politician. To help you do this, we are going to show you how tenure politics is often like the political give-and-take of a legislature.

Common myth holds that the academic tenure process is similar to a merit promotion system within a bureaucracy. Bureaucratic job descriptions are clearly defined and enumerated, criteria and standards for promotion are stated unambiguously, the evaluation of specific candidates is straightforward and apolitical, and outcomes are both fair and intuitively obvious. Some gaming may occur, but rules limit it. In merit-based bureaucracies, good candidates are promoted, weak candidates are not.

In reality, tenure politics is more like passing legislation. Legislatures are at times freewheeling, at other times hidebound with tradition. So is awarding tenure. In both awarding tenure and passing legislation, powerful key constituencies exert great influence. Both use peer decision. Both also use some form of majority rule and unrecorded or secret votes. Other similarities include the importance of political skills in both tenure and legislative processes, the common emphasis on information and image management, and the role in outcomes played by background similarity and informal network groups. In both settings, informal criteria may triumph over formal criteria. Participants may employ self-interested voting strategies to deflect threats to the status quo. And in each setting, money may play a role.

Let us briefly examine these similarities and what each means for managing your tenure case. We will see how two different tenure candidates, Political Paul and Naive Nancy, deal with the legislative character of tenure. Political Paul recognizes the legislative character of tenure. Naive Nancy assumes tenure to be an apolitical merit system in which she will automatically be rewarded if she does a good job. Paul is in the economics department of a small university. Nancy is in the biology department at the same place.

Your Colleagues and Tenure Politics

Tenure is partly political because the participation of your colleagues makes it so. (See Table 2.1.)

Key Constituencies: Caring About Your Tenure

Both the passage of a bill through a legislature and awarding academic tenure affect key constituencies beyond the immediately obvious. Plainly, bills are supported by their sponsors, who introduce them on behalf of home-district constituencies. Yet other constituencies and powerful groups are also affected. This includes similar constituencies in other districts, bureaucrats who must administer programs, and legislators who may be held publicly accountable for supporting the legislation. Interest groups who fear their own benefits will be reduced if legislation favoring some other group is passed are also concerned.

In granting tenure, why your tenure decision is important to you is obvious. But other "constituencies" also are affected by your tenure decision. Tenured faculty members in the same department may be concerned about the impact of your tenure on faculty turnover and the quality of the working atmosphere in the department. Here, through your actions and behavior, you must convince senior colleagues that your presence will have a positive impact on the working environment.

Granting you tenure also affects other untenured members in your department who anticipate going up for tenure in the near future. Heavily tenured departments may have either overt or hidden quotas on the percentage of faculty members who can be tenured. Awarding tenure to you may reduce the probability of concurrent or subsequent candidates receiving it. Competition among junior faculty members in a heavily tenured department may be worse if few retirements are anticipated in the immediate future. Also, some departments

Table 2.1 Your Colleagues and Tenure Politics

Powerful key constituencies care about your tenure.
 Strategy:
  Convince department members that you contribute to the depart-
   ment's working environment.
  Cooperate rather than compete directly with junior colleagues.
  Stay above the fray of departmental infighting.
  When possible, support the department chair's goals.
  Convince administrators you are a good tenure risk.
Peers decide your tenure outcome.
 Strategy:
  Do not rely on promises for protection from the chair.
  Build a tenurable record.
  Develop cordial relations with all department members.
The majority rules.
 Strategy:
  Count votes, because size of vote margin matters.
  Try to get a large positive vote in your department.
Individual votes are not public.
 Strategy:
  Begin open dialogue with department members who may not be
   initially supportive.
  Show skeptics how you are meeting criticism.
Informal criteria sometimes triumph over formal criteria.
 Strategy:
  Be sensitive to informal concerns as well as to formal criteria.
  Be aware of shifting or rising standards for excellence.
  Examine recent favorable cases as the best guidelines for what "now"
   means.
Your colleagues may use self-interested status quo voting strategies.
 Strategy:
  Avoid appearing either "too good" or "too bad."
  Downplay differences between your production and that of senior
   colleagues.
  Choose your job carefully so that performance expectations match
   your abilities.

---

feel they can only tenure one or two specialists in a particular
subfield. Cutthroat competition with other junior colleagues
is rarely beneficial in the long run. If you both make it through
tenure and you have alienated a junior colleague in the process,

you have made an enemy for life. You may need the support of other junior colleagues in research and teaching. Overt competition may convince senior colleagues that you are not a good department member. Just as in legislative settings, members act courtly and courteous toward each other, trading support on issues and bills; cooperation with other junior colleagues rather than head-to-head competition is a beneficial strategy.

The current department chair as well as department members who harbor ambitions to become chair are also affected by your tenure decision. In many research-oriented universities, serving as department chair is regarded as a burden and detraction from research. In other universities and some colleges, faculty members who have ambitions for administrative careers view service as department chair as a crucial stepping stone. Those ambitious to run the department may be interested in whether you support their candidacy for chair. If bitter fighting is going on over who will be chair, you are better off to stay above the fray and uninvolved. If relations are more cordial, support the goals of your chair when possible.

College administrators are also affected by your tenure decision. Besides the institutional multimillion-dollar financial commitment your tenure represents, deans like neither to alienate their faculty members by overriding faculty decisions too often nor to be overridden by higher-level administrators or boards of trustees. Most administrators want to tenure candidates who will not cause them trouble with other key constituencies with whom they must deal and who, by their subsequent performance and behavior, will make the administrator look good. Here you must convince your dean and other administrators that you are a good tenure risk.

Peers Deciding Your Tenure Outcome

In both tenure and legislatures, peer decisions rather than hierarchial or superior review are used at critical stages. Peer decisions are judgments of equals. In legislatures, this judgment occurs on the chamber floor. In tenure, the department decision is a peer decision. Like party leaders and committee chairs, academic department chairs are the "first among equals" in their ability to manipulate rewards, to persuade, and to influence. Neither department chairs nor legislative committee chairs can decree or command particular outcomes. Both types of leaders may be forced to accept group decisions when they personally prefer other alternatives. Rotating department chairs may have less influence than more permanent department heads. Regardless of which type you have, remember that your chair cannot circumvent peer decisions. You should not rely on promises from your chair to protect you at tenure time. Decentralized voting and peer review drive tenure-decision outcomes, and your chair may not be able to protect you even if he or she wants to. Spend your time building a tenurable record and cordial relations with all of your department colleagues.

The Majority Rules

Most legislatures use simple majority rule most of the time. Exceptions are overriding an executive veto or terminating a filibuster when extraordinary majorities are required. Tenure decisions are also based on majority rule, although the size of the majority required to pass forward a candidate's file for review at higher levels may vary across universities and colleges. In some colleges, a simple majority-favorable department vote is adequate to pass forward a candidate's file. In other colleges, majorities as large as two thirds of voting department members may be required.

Whatever the required majority, the size of the actual majority favoring approval matters. In legislatures, the greater the favorable majority, the smaller the probability of an executive veto. In your tenure, the greater the favorable margin in your department vote, the less likely your tenure will be overturned later by university committees, administrators,

or trustees. Be a vote counter! Try to get your margin of departmental approval as high as possible.

Individual Votes Are Not Public

Secrecy plays a role in both legislatures and tenure. While
a small percentage of legislative floor votes are recorded roll
calls, a much larger proportion of floor votes take place by
voice vote, with individual votes unrecorded. Many of the
trade-offs made in committees and bill formulation take place
in private. Similarly, secrecy plays an important role in tenure
decisions. In most departments, tenure votes are secret bal-
lots. Secrecy allows a senior department colleague to present
a public image either by statements or strategic silence of
supporting one position, while actually voting another position. Some colleges require that voting faculty members justify their decision in writing. The aim of this requirement is
to force voting members to justify their decisions by formal
tenure criteria. Yet these written justifications are not made
public, either to the tenure candidate or to other department
members. Thus, secrecy protects department members from
public accountability for how they vote.

There is not much you can do to change this aspect of tenure.
But you can develop open relations with department members who may not be initially supportive of you. If these department members feel they can discuss their true objections to
your tenure case with you openly, then you can begin a dialogue to show them your strategies for overcoming their criticisms and correcting any weaknesses about which they have
concern.

Informal Criteria: Triumph Over Formal Criteria?

The criteria for judging legislative bills are often vague.
Standards vary across sessions and chambers. Informal criteria often are different from and more important than stated

rationales. Public rationales include enhancing the public interest and promoting economic growth. Unstated, informal rationales, however, include the need to placate powerful special interest groups and bringing benefits home to key constituencies. Similar vagueness of standards helps separate formal from informal criteria in tenure decisions. Although the areas for excellence are clearly identified in most formal tenure procedures as research, teaching, and service, the specific achievements required for success in each area are rarely specified. What excellence means is left to interpretation in each specific tenure case. Excellence becomes whatever a majority of voting tenured faculty members in a particular department at a particular time say it is. Formal criteria may focus on the quality of your research and number of publications. Informal concerns include the impact of granting you tenure on departmental interest groups. Be sensitive to these informal concerns.

Because standards of excellence are not plainly stated, tenure standards may shift. Shifting standards are part of what makes political skills important in the tenure process. Sometimes shifting standards cause candidates to be treated unequally and unfairly. Less sociable, less likable tenure candidates may be rejected, while more sociable, more likable candidates with equal or inferior professional records may slide through. Be aware of shifting standards of excellence. Make sure you have examined recent cases of accepted candidates as the best guideline to what excellence means now.

Your Colleagues: Using Self-Interested Status Quo Voting Strategies

In legislatures, bills most likely to pass give rewards to some without taking away benefits from others. Such bills do not disturb the status quo in significant ways. Similarly, tenure is more likely if you do not appear to threaten the general status quo of power relationships within your department. Your chances are even brighter if you simultaneously offer specific contributions valued by some of your tenured colleagues. What you can contribute that is valued may vary by department. Some departments value a needed teaching specialty. Others appreciate cutting-edge research skills or national visibility in a certain subspecialty. If you know computer software and statistical skills and are willing to help fellow department members with their research, you are especially likely to be appreciated and valued.

In legislatures, members consider the impact of casting a particular vote on their own careers and power within the legislature. In tenure decisions, voting faculty may also develop self-interested voting strategies. A department chair may be concerned about the impact of the tenure candidacy on his attempts to consolidate a personal coalition within the department. Tenured faculty members may be concerned about keeping the share of untenured faculty constant as well as the impact of the tenure candidacy on future promotions and salary. Untenured faculty members may be concerned about maximizing their own chances of later obtaining tenure.

When self-interested voting strategies are blatantly applied in departments that have not held high performance standards in the past, productive tenure candidates may actually be penalized for being too good and thus being "rate busters." Low-producing, already tenured department members may be threatened by the implied rising expectations for research and publication if frequently publishing junior colleagues are tenured. Tenuring high producers changes the dynamics for distributing salary increases within the department by increasing the level of competition and expectations for doing well. Low producers used to coasting while collecting regular salary increases may fear that they will no longer be competitive for the highest raises. If you publish much more than your colleagues, you are advised to downplay the difference, at least until you are tenured. You do not want to be penalized for being "too good"! Being too good can sometimes be as hazardous to your tenure as being "too bad," given the realities of self-interested voting by tenured faculty. This means you are well advised to choose your place of employment carefully. Obviously, departments with standards so high you have no hope of meeting them are poor choices of places for employment. Less obviously, departments with standards so low that you threaten senior colleagues are also poor choices. When possible, choose a job where your colleagues' expectations match your abilities.

You and Tenure Politics

Some legislative facets of tenure can be directly managed by you and depend on your own political skill. (See Table 2.2.)

Polishing Your Political Skills

In legislatures, some bills have so little support that they stand little chance of passage from the beginning. A few others are so popular that they sail through the legislative process unimpeded and are passed unanimously. Most bills, however, fall between these two extremes so that the probability of passage depends to a great degree on the political skills of their sponsors and floor managers. Bills with skillful sponsors and floor managers will pass, and those with politically clumsy sponsors and disinterested floor managers will not.

Similarly, a small number of tenure candidates are widely perceived as so productive and brilliant that they easily pass through the tenure process. Another small number of candidates are widely perceived as inadequate, and they should be denied tenure. The great majority of tenure candidates, however, are in the wide territory between these two extremes. If you are in this middle ground, political skills and sensitivities are important. If you are politically skilled in building a supporting coalition, your probability of gaining tenure is enhanced. Two key strategies for building coalitions are showing shared interests and exchanging favors. You can build

Table 2.2 You and Tenure Politics

Polish your political skills.
> Strategy:
>> Build toward a supporting coalition.
>> Point out common interests and perspectives.
>> Exchange favors and professional courtesies.

Manage information about you and your professional image.
> Strategy:
>> Target information about your successes to faculty members most interested in that aspect of academics.
>> Manage your department image.
>> Downplay failures with humor.
>> Demonstrate modesty at successes.

Shared backgrounds help.
> Strategy:
>> Use similar backgrounds to begin effective communication.
>> Work extra hard to establish good communications if your background is dissimilar to your colleagues.
>> Do not highlight differences.
>> Minorities and women should seek out advice from senior colleagues who have similar backgrounds.

Money always matters.
> Strategy:
>> Even small grants are viewed favorably.
>> Large grants are even better, but do not flaunt your success.
>> Distribute grant funds to your department when possible.

---

toward a supporting coalition in your department through your willingness to help colleagues with small things that matter to them, such as covering a class when they must attend a professional meeting or bringing interesting scholarship to their attention. Point out common interests and perspectives on the field.

Managing Information About You and Your Professional Image

Floor managers of legislative bills disseminate different information to fellow legislators. Floor managers use discretion to determine what information, arguments, and incentives would be most effective among various legislators, tailoring the approaches used for each. You may pursue a similar strategy of information dissemination and image management at work. For example, target information about your teaching skills and interest to colleagues most concerned with teaching. In the years before you go up for tenure, give copies of your relevant publications and conference papers to colleagues who are concerned with and interested in research and scholarship. Downplay failures with humor, place positive interpretations on ambiguous information, discreetly disseminate information about successes, and respond to praise with appropriate modesty.

The Value of Shared Backgrounds

For legislators, similar backgrounds affect friendship patterns, information channels, and group cohesion, as well as increase the cohesiveness needed to pass bills. Dissimilar backgrounds reduce the probability of collegiality, friendship, and informal information dissemination. Greater work is needed to achieve cohesiveness. Similarity of backgrounds is also a factor in academic tenure decisions, although its role is rarely acknowledged publicly. If you have an educational and personal background similar to your department colleagues, prospects for friendship and information sharing are enhanced. Although these do not translate directly into a positive tenure vote, they are compatible with a favorable outcome. If you have a similar background with department colleagues, use it as a departure point for talking about professional interests. If you are dissimilar in background, work extra hard to develop good communication with your colleagues. Do not highlight your differences except in rare instances.

In legislatures, women and minority members in the past were often precluded from the proverbial back rooms where hard negotiations occurred. Gender and racial differences worked against immediate entry into the informal power structure. Persons with unusual life-styles, accents, habits of dress, and intellectual perspectives also may be separated from the mainstream and its informal information channels. In universities, the numbers of women and minorities who have gained tenure have increased somewhat in recent years, although both groups remain much smaller proportions of the tenured professoriate than among either the general population or college graduates. If you fall in one of these underrepresented categories, seek out a senior person similar to yourself to provide perspective on how to best manage your tenure case. But do not be afraid to heed the well-founded advice of senior colleagues who are white males.

Money: It Always Matters

Legislators are esteemed by their proximity to money. Members of finance and appropriations committees involved with raising and spending funds have greater influence than those more removed from money. Legislators who bring home financial benefits to district constituencies are viewed more favorably than those who not. Leaders who raise campaign funds for rank-and-file members are more beloved than those who do not.

Similarly, in tenure, bringing money in to your university will generate approval. Tenure candidates who have been successful at getting grants are more beloved than those who have shown little interest or ability in raising funds. Even small grants increase your colleagues' esteem of you. You must be careful, however, to not flaunt success at getting large grants. You do not want to inspire jealousy, only admiration.

University or college rules often dictate the internal distribution of overhead funds within the institution. Whenever possible, consider distributing some of the benefits of successful fund raising to department colleagues. You might help your department by writing into your grant proposals department benefits to be shared by all. This may include enhanced secretarial support, telephones, and travel money.

You may also include direct salary funds for summer or overload payments for some department faculty members.

Political Paul Versus Naive Nancy

Consider how Paul behaved in the years before his tenure decision. He was aware of the importance of his tenure decision to others. In his department, a powerful senior faculty member who specialized in trade economics wanted to challenge the current chair, a microtheory specialist. Loose coalitions were forming, but despite collaborating on two articles with a senior faculty member in the potential challenger's coalition, Paul remained distantly friendly with members of both coalitions. He made a special effort to go to lunch regularly with members of the chair's coalition, even though that faction was characterized as "less current" in modern econometric techniques. He served on department and college committees when asked by the chair and made a point of reporting back to the chair what went on in committee meetings. As a connoisseur of campus politics, the chair was grateful for the blow-by-blow accounts.

Paul also worked amicably with one of the other two junior faculty members in the department. Even though Paul had a superior record, he did not inspire envy among his younger colleagues. He provided statistical advice to the junior colleague with whom he did not collaborate, as well as to some senior colleagues. Paul often told mild "PG-rated" jokes at lunch, and others enjoyed dropping by his office for a chat. At one point, Paul sensed that two older faculty members were not supportive of him. He made a special effort to read articles in their areas of expertise and to discuss the findings with these senior colleagues. Although he never became close friends with these colleagues, they developed a respect for his knowledge of the literature.

One year Paul had a problem with an undergraduate class. For some reason, the class did not respond well to his teaching methods. Five students sat in the back and distracted other students. Their cynicism spread throughout the class. Paul's teaching reviews were much lower for that class than normal. He did not discuss the evaluations openly at lunch but instead wrote a memo for his chair and his annual review file stating not only the factors contributing to the lower-than-normal evaluations but also the strategies he would adopt the next time he taught the class. Paul's chair was impressed with his concern and thoughtfulness. Paul also quickly discovered that he rarely got an article accepted on the first try. Although he would joke in the abstract about the trials of the peer-review process, he did not discuss each rejection with the lunch group. Instead he discussed strategies for revisions with his collaborators and his former adviser from graduate school.

Paul's colleagues perceived Paul as a solid department citizen. He received a favorable tenure vote with a comfortable margin of support.

Nancy had always been a straight-A student, even in graduate school. She had won national fellowships in which her natural brightness and analytic capacity were automatically recognized. Unlike Paul, Nancy had never been involved in student politics. Casual chatting and banter did not come easily to her. She often worked in her office with her door closed, so her colleagues were frequently not even aware that she was in the department. Nancy's chair had asked her to serve on two committees. She agreed to serve on one, but the meeting times of the other interfered with her laboratory work so she declined. She continued to work with her dissertation adviser from graduate school, but coauthored only one conference paper with someone from her new department. That person left after a three-year appointment and was not at the university when Nancy's tenure decision was made. Much of Nancy's research was quite complicated. Because no one in Nancy's department worked in the same area, she rarely discussed her work while at school. Nancy felt that her work was good and that she was better than the other junior colleague in the department, but she tried to hide this attitude.

Most of her colleagues were not sure what Nancy did most of the time. The idea that she would have to count tenure votes was repulsive to her, because she felt she had enough peer-reviewed articles to merit a positive tenure outcome. Nancy had applied for a National Institutes of Health (NIH) grant, but it had not gotten funding on the first round. She planned to apply again. When she was getting the grant ready, she did spend a lot of time in the department, so that her colleagues were aware of her application. When they inquired about the outcome, she said it did not get funding, without explaining that NIH grants often do not receive funding on their first submission.

When Nancy went up for tenure, her colleagues could see that she had enough publications, but they were not sure about the quality of her work and the journals in which she had published, because they did not work in that field. Her teaching evaluations were average, despite her hard work in lab sections, because she was not a dynamic speaker. Her tenure vote was very close. Fortunately, she had continued to work with her adviser, who had included Nancy on grants funded by drug companies. Although Nancy had not perceived a need to do so, her adviser had written in benefits for Nancy's department into the grant. This, plus the number of publications she had published, finally persuaded some department members to support her. She squeaked through the tenure decision by the skin of her teeth.

Nancy was fortunate that her relationships with her colleagues, while distant, were not hostile and that the department was not fighting. If members had been in competing coalitions, her tenure outcome may well have been different. Given how marginal and unenthusiastic her unit support was, a politically divided department, coupled with her general lack of political sensitivity, may have been her downfall. Fortunately, her department colleagues had cordial relations with one another, and Nancy's adviser was more politically skilled than was she. Recognizing her abilities, he continued to function as a mentor interested in her career long after her departure from graduate school. This was lucky for Nancy. As it was, her lack of political skills helped make a solid case for tenure into a squeaker.

3 | The Prologue to Tenure

It is never too early to begin to prepare for moving through the tenure process. Most graduate students begin thinking about tenure when they take their first academic job, if not before. In fact, as the preceding chapters indicate, it is important to think about tenure when choosing a job. Landing a tenure-track job soon after completion of the Ph.D. is a high priority for most scholars who aspire to an academic career. Our goal here is to describe the tenure process during the probationary years as an assistant professor—a six-year period in most cases.

Although the tenure process varies across universities and from university to college, many steps are similar across institutions. We explore the general process found at most institutions, as well as some of the major variants, especially in key decision makers in different locales. We also follow the timing and sequencing of important events in the tenure process. In the next two chapters we trace decisions and activities from the initial appointment at the university or college in a tenure-track position to the year before going up for tenure and, finally, waiting for the process to be over. One assumption made by savvy junior faculty members is that it is never too early to begin to prepare for the tenure process. We hope to demystify that process and to provide practical tips on what to think about and what to prepare for at each step.

36

Completing the Ph.D.
Completing a postdoctoral degree in some scientific and applied fields
Landing a tenure-track job
Marking an acceptable amount of time on the tenure clock
Getting interim contracts totaling six years
The tenure decision and promotion to associate professor
Promotion from associate to full professor rank
Being awarded an endowed chair

Figure 3.1. Academic Career Gateposts

Academic Career Gateposts

In the course of your academic career as a faculty member, you must pass by several "gateposts," not unlike horses in a race passing gateposts. For newly recruited professors, tenure is a crucial career gatepost. Indeed, it is the biggest gatepost in an academic career. Several gateposts, however, precede tenure. (See Figure 3.1.)

Completing the Ph.D.

If you want an academic career, in all but a few fields you must first successfully complete a Ph.D. program in a relevant field at a recognized university. If you are working toward your Ph.D. and have completed everything but your dissertation, your status is called "ABD" ("all but dissertation"). Because teaching new courses for the first time can be stressful and time-consuming, your Ph.D. adviser may encourage you to complete your dissertation before leaving your Ph.D. institution. If you have defended your dissertation before physically leaving graduate school, you can plunge into the rigors of your new job, especially compiling a tenurable record, without the angst of your dissertation hanging over your head. You may also begin using your dissertation to create a publishing record.

You may not have the luxury, however, of finishing the dissertation before launching your working career. Financial pressures, family issues, or a need to move with a spouse may dictate that you launch into teaching at a new university before defending your dissertation. ABD candidates who do land tenure-track jobs are expected to complete their dissertations shortly after arriving at their tenure-track jobs. You, too, are well advised to finish the dissertation post haste. Failing to do so can result in dismissal from your first job and will likely derail your career.

Landing a Tenure-Track Job

Before you can even compete for tenure, you must first land a tenure-track job. Not all jobs within academics include the right to earn tenure. Some full-time jobs are temporary or short-term appointments. Recruits who fill these jobs understand their appointment is only for a year or two years or possibly even just a semester. Likely such jobs are as replacements for tenured faculty members who have gone on leave and who retain the right to come back to their university after their sabbatical or leave without pay. Other teaching jobs that carry expectations of clinical duties or training of nontraditional students not enrolled in regular degree programs may also not be tenure-track and therefore may not include the right to compete for tenure. Many universities increasingly use adjunct professors to teach part-time loads of one or more courses. Adjunct professorships also are not typically tenure-track.

When you go on the job market, you should identify whether a particular position is tenure-track on the initial job interview or even before. Rarely are jobs that are not tenure-track converted to tenure-track status when someone is already employed in the position. Even if such a conversion were to take place, rules put forth by the AAUP designate that tenure-track positions should be advertised nationally in a fair and open process. Thus a conversion would likely require a new national search. You may not get the converted position, even though you are currently meeting the job duties. Department politics and other factors beyond your control may have a significant impact.

Marking an Acceptable Amount of Time on the "Tenure Clock"

AAUP guidelines on the "tenure clock" followed by most major state and private universities embrace the concept of "up or out" in seven years. This timeline is designed to provide new faculty members with enough time to prove their professorial worth and yet provide some assurance of commitment by the institution in a not overly long period of time. Once on a tenure-track job, your "tenure clock" begins ticking. You must either be given tenure (up) or else must leave the institution (out), vacating the tenure-track position in seven years. Because the tenure decision itself takes a year, and professors who are dismissed must be given a year's notice, you basically have five years to produce a tenurable record of achievement.

Universities and colleges differ in whether any time you spend in a tenure-track job before the dissertation is completed is "counted" on the tenure clock. Some colleges do not start the tenure clock until you defend your dissertation and earn your Ph.D. Others will give you the option of counting or not counting predissertation-defense job time toward tenure clock time. If you have not completed your dissertation, you may be given the rank of instructor. Once the dissertation is completed, you will be promoted to the rank of assistant professor.

If you are anxious, you may find the tenure clock very slow and the current tenure process agonizingly long. The actual time to tenure is nevertheless highly compressed in terms of granting such a major benefit (lifetime job security) based on an employment record of six or fewer years. The tenure timetable definitely works in the favor of self-starters who produce much and quickly, often with minimal guidance. It works against slow starters and late bloomers who may need more guidance or who may have false starts on various research projects that do not pan out.

Recognizing the highly constrained timeframe for earning tenure once the tenure clock has been started, some schools allow the clock to be "stopped" for promising candidates who made need extra time. In the biological and physical sciences, postdoctoral studies, called "postdocs," are common. Postdocs are one- or two-year jobs at a junior status that may be taken so that you can work on research teams with well-known scholars at major universities after you have completed your dissertation and before you take your first tenure-track job. If you get a postdoc, you will likely be paid from grants and other income the senior professor you work with has brought into his or her university. During the postdoc, you may expand your skills and work on research for publication without the stress of also teaching new courses for the first time. The effect of the postdoc is to expand the number of years between graduate school and when you must go up for tenure.

At some universities with medical schools and the sciences, the number of promising candidates for tenure may exceed the tenure-track slots. Such schools keep junior candidates on a "collateral" track until a tenure-track position opens up. Other times, candidates who have heavy clinical, administrative, or service loads that reduce their research productivity may be temporarily moved to a collateral track for a year or two to "stop the tenure clock" while publishable research is produced. Critics of this system contend that collateral tracks have the potential for becoming "ghettos" for women and minorities, while white males gain access to tenure-track positions more readily. Collateral tracks do sometimes, however, serve as a cushion for professors doing good work but not falling exactly within the six-year tenure timeframe. Still other reasons for stopping the tenure clock include taking a leave of absence. If you receive a national fellowship, a maternity or health leave, or a leave to conduct field research or to teach abroad for a year or more, you may have the option of stopping the tenure clock. Tenure clocks are specific to individual universities and colleges. However, universities and colleges may exercise discretion as to whether to let you count previous years of employment at other schools on your own tenure clock. With such discretion, if you need more time before tenure to compile a suitable record, you may disregard prior employment at other institutions.

Interim Employment Contracts

During the time you are an assistant professor, you may have several contracts for one or more years of employment. How many contracts you get and how long each one is may vary. Usually, the total number of years for the contracts up until a tenure decision is made adds up to six years. The total of six pretenure years coincides with the amount of time a college has to decide whether to give you tenure, according to AAUP rules. In addition, if you are denied tenure, you are given a terminal year contract for a total of seven years. (See Figure 3.2.)

In some settings, getting your employment contract renewed before your tenure decision is an important gatepost. In settings where two 3-year contracts are given prior to the tenure decision, you may have to undergo a major peer review before the second 3-year contract is given. At this point, your tenured department colleagues may review evidence of your scholarship, teaching, and service. If they judge that you have little prospect of earning tenure in the remaining time before your tenure clock expires, you may not be renewed and may have to seek employment elsewhere.

Schools that use the contract renewal as a major career gatepost operate under the philosophy that it is better to dismiss quickly young professors who show little signs after three or four years of acquiring a tenurable record. These schools contend that tenure is a false hope if you have little chance of a positive tenure decision; waiting until your tenure decision

Possible pretenure decision contracts in years
Six 1-year contracts
Three 2-year contracts
Two 3-year contracts

Figure 3.2. Marking Time on the Tenure Clock

to find this out is more traumatic in the long run and keeps you from finding another job where the fit is better. This strategy allows young faculty members who are likely to be dismissed to look for another job without the stigma of having undergone a tenure rejection. Some schools also believe that although early dismissal of unpromising candidates does not rule out lawsuits from those who are dismissed, it does lower their probability.

Two commonly used models are one-year appointments with annual reviews and multiyear contracts with critical review periods. Both models assume a clear system of annual or periodic reviews. If your unit does not have a clear process of review and feedback (other than contract renewal), push for some type of review and feedback. You need advice from the department or at least the department chair. Even if an annual report of your activities is not required, provide it to the chair and ask for feedback. It is better to hear negative comments and ways to change in the third year of appointment and be able to follow the advice than to hear through the grapevine in the summer before the sixth year that you should have published in different places, done a bit more service, and tried to improve your teaching ratings.

Other variations in appointment contracts are less common but possible. One that almost never occurs is an initial appointment to a seven-year contract, with no formal review prior to the tenure decision in the sixth year. Many universities provide only one-year contracts, with varying amounts and degree of formality of review for each year's renewal.

Even with one-year contracts, almost all universities renew almost everyone for a second year. One year is too soon to judge a person on teaching or scholarship. In a system of one-year contracts, the first important decision may be during the middle of the second year. It occurs then rather than in the spring, because the general AAUP guidelines are that during the second year of appointment a faculty member must be notified of nonreappointment by December 15 of the academic year ending in May. After two years of appointment, the general norm is that a faculty member will receive a full year's notice (and thus be at the university for one more full academic year) if he or she is not reappointed. Often the most important review periods are years 4 and 5 (those periods close to the tenure-review year). By that point, your record should be forming well.

Reviews with few criticisms are a sign that you should receive tenure. Reviews with many critical statements (for example, you need to increase your rate and quality of publication or you need to pay more attention to developing a record of consistent publication as well as improve your classroom teaching skills) are a warning sign of serious problems. The on-time, steady producer described in a later chapter will generally have always received positive statements in reviews (for example, viewed as a steady and consistent publisher, growing academic reputation, good teacher, and good department citizen).

Some universities have a system of critical review periods that often are combined with multiyear contracts. In this system, no review may be conducted in the first or even second year. Most typical is a review at the end of the second year to decide whether to renew the first three-year contract. Often the next two renewals are for two years each. A low producer on scholarship or a person completely ineffective in the classroom might not be renewed at this point. More typically, the assistant professor will receive a two-year renewal but with comments about ways to improve (increase rate of publication, increase quality of publication, concentrate publication in a few areas to improve academic reputation, improve teaching). Some comments of needed improvement are typical at this point in the career, even for an on-time steady producer. At this stage, departments often believe they should be providing career advice.

The second hurdle is often a fourth-year review with three different outcomes: (a) a decision not to reappoint, (b) a conditional renewal (in some places with only a one-year contract and an additional review in the spring of the fifth year immediately prior to the tenure-decision year), and (c) a two-year renewal without conditions. The renewal without conditions usually indicates that a person is progressing well toward tenure and should "make it" if rates of productivity and teaching quality do not change. A conditional renewal at this point is very serious. Pay close attention to the criticisms. You generally must meet them to receive tenure in your sixth year. If you consider some criticisms unfair or some goals unattainable, then discuss these with your chair. You may be able to modify the department's expectations or better explain your own record and accomplishments.

Learning the Rules Early

The first piece of advice for this stage of the career is to get started immediately! Find out right away what the written and unwritten rules are at your university. The best place to begin this process is with your department chair. Developing colleagues, both junior and senior, with whom to compare notes is also helpful. Most universities and colleges have written criteria for tenure and promotion. In that case, pay attention to what is listed and use those criteria as a way to plan both your activity and your strategy for documenting your case some years hence. Although AAUP rules specify the maximum time a candidate may take before going up for tenure, informal norms may specify the minimum. Some universities almost never allow a candidate to be tenured "early," and even suggesting such a decision may be interpreted as a sign of arrogance by colleagues. Even mentioning the possibility of early promotion and tenure should be explored carefully (preferably with faculty in other departments to acquire some sense of institutional norms). Junior faculty members who have had spectacular early careers may desire to go up for tenure early. When going up early, it is always better to be encouraged to do so by others and to have the support of the chair. Often candidates who go up early are expected to have especially strong records, stronger than they would have needed if they had waited until it was their "tenure-decision" or "up-or-out" year. Also, an early promotion and tenure decision may set future expectations of extremely high rates of productivity for the faculty member as long as he or she remains in that university. Thus the early promotion decision may, in effect, "up the ante" for promotion to full professor in five or six years beyond the minimum criteria.

The Tenure Decision

The tenure decision constitutes a major career gatepost. Candidates typically put themselves forward for tenure and for promotion from assistant to associate professor at the same time. Most successful candidates receive both tenure and promotion at the same time. In some early cases, however, the candidate may receive only the promotion and be required to resubmit the file the next year to be approved for tenure.

A particularly rare decision is one to grant tenure but not promotion. Such decisions occur when candidates are perceived to be weak. Although decision makers in the tenure process do not wish to force the candidate receiving this mixed decision to leave the university, they also wish to withhold promotion until greater productivity is displayed.

Generally, however, most faculty of associate professor rank also have tenure. One exception may occur when a professor leaves one university or college for employment in another tenure-granting institution. Tenure is institution-specific. Some but not all colleges and universities will hire senior faculty members who have been granted tenure at other institutions without forcing them to resubmit to a lengthy formal tenure-review process. Some colleges and universities, but not all or even many, refuse to grant tenure to a recently hired faculty member without a probationary period, even if that faculty member has an impressive record at another institution and within the field generally.

In such cases, recently hired associate and even full professors may not have tenure the first years of their employment in their new institutions. Rather, they are required to submit a tenure file after a probationary period has been fulfilled. This period is typically shorter (often three years) for associate professors than the normal probationary period for assistant professors. For full professors, the probationary period may be as short as one year.

Tenure is important, because if you fail to get tenure in the allowable time, you are dismissed. If you earn tenure, you get to keep the job you have. This up-or-out character of tenure is similar to the promotion system used in U.S. military services, where officers must make the next rank within a specified timeframe or else be mustered out. Soldiers who are mustered out for failing to make the next rank in a timely manner must necessarily return to civilian life. Professors who are essentially mustered out of their professorial jobs because they are denied tenure can always go to another university or college and start the tenure clock all over again. Our aim is to provide enough information about the tenure process and tips about how to put your best case forward so that you succeed on your first try.

4 | Stepping Through the Tenure Process

This chapter explores the time immediately before your tenure decision and the actual process by which tenure is decided. We will examine who makes the tenure decision, its timeframe, and how you prepare your tenure file.

Who Makes the Tenure Decision?

The Unit Decision

Universities and colleges vary in who has authority to make the tenure decision. Usually, however, only tenured faculty members of higher rank in your own unit will make the initial decision. The definition of unit can vary from a traditional disciplinary department in most larger universities to a multidisciplinary unit covering all social sciences or humanities in some smaller colleges. In some applied fields, such as schools of social work or education, the relevant "unit" may consist of the entire school-level faculty.

The senior faculty members in the unit are generally considered to be the people with the best knowledge of your academic area. They are felt to have the best understanding of the time demands for research and teaching in the field. These senior members are also viewed as knowing the importance of service in the academic area, the prestige of journal outlets and other publication choices, and the significance of meeting presentations. In some units, a specific vote count is taken, and in others consensus is limited to a recommendation and forwarded letter.

The Department Chair's Recommendation

The department chair's letter is often the next decision step in the process. Your department chair will generally write a letter that is forwarded to the dean of the college (or the unit head of the next administrative level in more unusual settings). Your department chair may or may not agree with the rest of the faculty. In some universities, department chairs are not allowed to be in the general unit meeting to discuss the tenure candidate. In others, the chair can attend the tenure meeting and present his or her views but cannot vote because of his or her separate vote as chair.

Along with the faculty, the opinion of your chair usually counts heavily at higher levels. Because your chair, like the rest of the faculty, is in the same academic discipline, he or she is considered to be quite knowledgeable about what is good and bad work. In addition, your chair is expected to take an overall view that is concerned about the department's well-being and to focus on unit needs. Thus your chair's letter can be very helpful in explaining certain negative comments from faculty or several negative votes. If the chair explains that the negative comments are linked to some long-standing divisions within the department, then such comments and votes may be discounted at higher levels.

Because your chair's opinion stands out in the process as compared to other faculty members, it is important to develop a feeling for whether he or she is supportive. Although some candidates achieve tenure over the opposition of their department chair, the process runs more smoothly if he or she is supportive. You need to pay special attention to what the chair values and how he or she views the process. Because your chair is the unit's administrative leader, find out early in your career his or her understanding of the tenure process and what tips the chair recommends. Take advantage of yearly performance reviews to discuss your progress with the chair. If your unit does not mandate annual reviews, then ask your chair to provide them. Use these sessions as an opportunity to get to know the chair and to learn his or her opinion of how the department values different types of activities. Also, both in a review session and throughout the year, keep your chair and other key faculty members informed of your activities. Tell them when a paper is accepted for presentation or publication. Ask which of your activities are viewed favorably and should continue, and what the chair would like to see you change.

Decision Points Outside the Unit

Beyond the department chair, different tenure-review structures abound. One model is a review committee of nonadministrative faculty at the school level. This committee makes a recommendation to the dean, who then recommends the case up the administrative ladder (provost, president, board of trustees). Another model is that of the administrative ladder only, starting with the dean and proceeding upward. A third model is the presence of a faculty oversight committee at a higher administrative level than the school, often university- or college-wide in scope. This committee may review files before the provost or between provost and president. Faculty oversight committees often operate differently than administrators (deans, provosts, and university presidents). Generally, the charge for a faculty review committee is (a) to be sure any written rules and procedures are followed and, at times (b), to make an independent judgment of quality. If the faculty oversight committee only reviews process, any questions raised are made either in a special note in the file or the file is returned to the unit for reconsideration. In universities in which the faculty oversight committee makes an independent judgment of quality, because the committee has faculty from different areas, determination of the best work is difficult. Often the letters from external reviewers become the most important part of the process at this stage. The opinion of these outside experts will receive great attention. Even at the beginning of a career, it is not too early to start to consider who might provide these external reviews. Who knows and respects your scholarly work? You might build on this knowledge for future use.

In contrast to faculty committees, administrators may often factor in issues such as the importance of the area of study, opinions about the overall quality of work in the department, concerns about too high a proportion of the department being tenured, or other issues with administrative impact. Most often, deans will agree with the department and chair, especially if the chair has kept the dean informed of the process and is a good politician within the unit. If the department committee and chair disagree, the dean has more latitude to make a separate decision, but in general deans most often side with chairs. The general proclivity of deans to back their chairs is another reason why having the chair on a candidate's side is good politics in the tenure process.

Provosts and presidents rarely form separate judgments about a particular candidate's scholarship, although they generally will have an opinion as to the quality of the department and its importance to the university mission. If the candidate's department is viewed as strong on campus, a positive recommendation from the unit will rarely be overturned at administrative levels. When positive unit recommendations are overturned at administrative levels, a major explanation

Board of trustees
President
Provost
Campuswide faculty review committee
Dean
School or college faculty review committee
Department or unit chair
Your unit or department

Figure 4.1. Who Makes the Tenure Decision?

is often that the provost considers the unit academically weak or unimportant to the overall goals and mission of the college or university.

If the unit is viewed as weak, the positive vote of the faculty and chair will carry less weight at high administrative levels. The evaluation of outside referees will attain even greater importance in those cases. Thus candidates who know their own departments' reputations to be weak should understand the tenure standards in stronger departments on campus and use those more stringent standards as guidelines rather than the weaker standards from their own departments. In such cases, a particularly strong individual record coupled by good outside letters from respected institutions is even more important than usual.

If the unit is viewed as unimportant for the university or college, very different factors may come into play in evaluating a tenure candidate. There is little a new faculty member can do to overcome the bias of being employed in a unit perceived by key decision makers as unimportant. *Before* the appointment is the time to avoid a possible negative outcome driven in large part by having an appointment in a unit unimportant to the institution. (See Figure 4.1.)

Getting Ready

During your probationary period as an assistant professor, there are several things you can do to help your tenure case. The year before tenure is especially important.

Retain Records of Relevant Activities

Throughout your entire period of pretenure contracts, retain information that indicates your levels of activity and success in teaching, research, and service. Sometimes at tenure time colleges require information on the actual courses you have taught each semester, the number of students enrolled, the number of independent studies, and sometimes even the titles of the projects supervised. Information is also required about the graduate student examination, thesis, and dissertation committees on which the tenure candidate has served. Similarly, keep records of publications, the aspect of record keeping most faculty do best even without thinking ahead. Documentation of all presentations at meetings and all types of service activities is also needed. Table 4.1 documents some of the types of activities about which you need to retain records. More details on these categories are discussed in the chapters on teaching, research, and service.

Some universities require details on personal performance and productivity each year in an annual report used for an annual review. If so, keep the annual reviews; thus most of the tedium of collecting specifics in the actual tenure decision year will have been accomplished. Save the material over the course of the year, either using your own unit's forms or the recommended items from Table 4.1. Keeping good records and saving materials are probably the most important pieces of advice at this early stage of a career. Without good records, five years later it will be very hard to document or even remember all of the independent studies, meeting presentations, and presentations to community groups that a tenure candidate may have made. Candidates with good, detailed

Table 4.1 Sample of Record Keeping in Teaching, Research, and Service

Teaching:
    Keep a count of each course taught by semester and enrollment (some universities also request numbers of withdrawals).
    List grade distributions for each course.
    Remember to keep count of independent study courses and senior honors theses or master's theses and dissertations directed.

Research:
    Maintain a current list of each published article on your CV.
    Keep a copy of each article in a publication file.
    List each article submitted and its progress.
    List meeting presentations (probably should be a section on your CV).
    List each grant submitted and the outcome of the review process.

Service:
    General department service
    Academic department service (being on master's and dissertation committees)
    College- or university-level service
    Activity in community organizations or committees
    Speeches to community groups
    Speeches to alumni groups
    Speeches to local practitioner associations (in practice-oriented fields)
    Activities in professional associations

records will be able to demonstrate more activity in each criterion area, even if they did not actually perform more activity.

Searching for Written Statements of Criteria

Ask about written statements of tenure criteria and auxiliary forms early. Institutions that have written criteria also often provide information forms and supporting materials. Try to look at a copy of this material (sometimes in a faculty tenure and promotion guide book or a faculty handbook) early in your career. Doing so can help you decide what kinds of information to retain. It can also give important clues as to the different activities that count in any university or college.

Both the specifics of written criteria and tenure forms vary across institutions. At some universities, criteria specify types of teaching, such as undergraduate, graduate, independent study, thesis committee, dissertation committee member, chairing a thesis committee or dissertation, development of new courses, and attendance of professional seminars linked to teaching. Generally, if the criteria are very specific about types of acceptable or expected activities, there are also specific forms to be used during the tenure year that match the more detailed criteria.

In other departments, the criteria may be very general or even unwritten. Forms are also typically general in such settings (outstanding teaching, excellence in teaching, etc.). Often less specified criteria mean a less formalized process at other steps, such as form preparation. See Table 4.2 for examples of specific and nonspecific criteria.

In the case of generalized criteria, terms are often used such as *excellent, good,* or *average* without definition being provided. Thus if you find such criteria in your unit, you will still need to find out how these terms are really interpreted.

The Year Before Tenure

A few short hints are important for this year. Be aware of time. Plan where you send your articles so that you will have responses back in time for the preparation of the tenure file, especially if you have been told you "need more articles" to have a good case. It may even be worth the effort to send a few articles to places known for rapid response on reviews and short time periods until publication. This will help you to avoid the appearance of "tenure busting"—that is, too many articles appearing in the year you are up for tenure. Finish up old projects and write up results rather than begin new long-term projects (although having an idea of a future research direction to discuss is positive). Save the beginning of a new project for the future. Think about holes in your record this year while you can still fill them, such as adding community

Table 4.2 Examples of Tenure and Promotion Criteria

I. Minimum Specificity
   A. For promotion to associate professor and tenure or tenure at the level of associate professor, a faculty member must be outstanding in scholarship for the stage of career and excellent in either teaching or service with the other level satisfactory. For promotion to full professor, a faculty member must be outstanding in scholarship (appropriate to the more senior stage of career, which generally includes at least one published book beyond the dissertation as well as publications in peer-reviewed journals) and outstanding in either teaching or service with the other area excellent.

II. Detailed Specificity
   A. There are three critical areas in the assessment of the suitability of a faculty member for tenure and promotion to associate professor: scholarship, teaching, and service.
      1. Scholarship: This is the most important of the three areas for tenure. The faculty member must:
         a. Provide evidence of written scholarship reviewed by peers, as in peer-reviewed journals or books from scholarly presses.
            i. Although specific numbers cannot be given, fewer than six to eight peer-reviewed articles will present a problem unless offset by book-length publications.
         b. Provide evidence of other written scholarship, such as in nonpeer-reviewed journals, edited collections, and books other than textbooks (which are considered evidence of service and improvement of teaching, but not scholarship). Publications in this area may enhance but not substitute for accomplishments in area 1 above.
         c. Provide evidence of attempts to obtain external and internal support for research and scholarly activities.
         d. As demonstration of scholarship in progress, presentations at professional meetings will be viewed as movement toward scholarly goals.
      2. Teaching: This is also a critical area of accomplishment for a faculty member. The member must:
         a. Provide evidence of the quantity of all types of teaching during the probationary period.
            i. Teaching of a reduced number of courses from the typical load should be explained as resulting from either the choice of department chair or the buyout of courses from external funding.

Table 4.2 (Continued)

ii. Nonassigned teaching (independent studies, honors theses, and chairing of master's and dissertation committees) should be included as evidence of quantity of teaching.

b. Provide evidence of quality of teaching through both the inclusion of student ratings completed in class and colleague observation. Student letters on quality of teaching may be included, but large numbers of these are discouraged.

i. Student ratings must be included for each course. In general, the faculty member should always be judged a satisfactory teacher (rating of 3) and preferably a good or excellent teacher. Substantial numbers of ratings below satisfactory are unacceptable for tenure and promotion, and such discrepancies in quality should be detailed by the candidate, colleague reviewers, and department chair.

ii. Colleague observation for at least two sessions of one course a year should be presented. Preferably, multiple courses should be observed in the final year before tenure, and by multiple colleague observers. Again, performance should be judged at least satisfactory and preferably as good or excellent.

c. Provide evidence of continued attention to improvement of teaching through attendance at university or professional didactic seminars, work on computer-based learning modules, or development of other student-oriented material, including textbooks and test files.

3. Service: Although this is the least critical area of accomplishment for promotion to associate professor, some evidence of service to the department, college, and university is required. Similarly, every candidate should evidence some commitment to professional service to the discipline and concern about the broader community and its needs. It should be noted in this regard that provision of talks or materials to a community group for which compensation is received, while noted as some activity with the community, is not deemed as service.

a. Provide evidence of department service each year and some service to the college or university.

b. Provide evidence of professional service to the discipline, preferably at the national or regional level and in increasingly visible positions over time.

c. Provide evidence of concern about the broader community as evidence by public talks, interviews with media, presentations to alumni groups, or service on local or state committees in the area of professional expertise.

service, working with a doctoral student, or conducting independent-study courses. Think about what you will teach and try to avoid a new teaching assignment or a course in which your evaluations are lower than for most of your other courses. Lastly, avoid conflict and fights, especially over relatively minor issues. Avoiding fights is always good advice, but its value is even greater this year and the next. In the year before the tenure decision, managing your image in the department and the college is particularly important. Do not give your colleagues a reason to dislike you or not care about your future.

Preparing the Tenure File and Materials

At most universities and colleges, a candidate for tenure must prepare a tenure file. Preparation typically includes completing a special form. Materials supporting the information on the form must be collected and presented, including teaching ratings (and often enrollment numbers), all published and submitted articles and sometimes work in progress, meeting papers, and documentation of special service or other activities, such as letters of appreciation or thanks for community presentations or help with some community group or professional board. In addition, at most universities, two other parts of the file are a personal statement and letters from external referees.

The Forms and Supporting Documentation

At most tenure-granting institutions, material supplied by the candidate is due at the beginning of the fall semester or in the early fall of the tenure decision year. Thus, file preparation may be an important activity of that summer. No matter how much the preparation of the form and pulling lots of supporting documents from files sounds like drudgery (for good reason—it is), do not avoid or ignore it. Preparing the tenure file and including an updated curriculum vita and a personal statement is most important.

Once the candidate's case moves beyond the department and chair level, the formal written file rather than personal interactions and familiarity with the candidate is what key decision makers will judge. Higher-level administrators and faculty from other departments serving on key committees may not know the candidate personally, especially in larger universities. Thus the appearance of the tenure file counts. Be neat, be complete, and follow directions. To the best you can, try to have something listed under each category on the tenure form.

Expect file preparation to take time. If you have gradually pulled materials over a month and have already completed yearly reports with most of the needed tenure material, the total time may be only a week. If you have not kept up with your own activities and documentation, the process could take much longer. Whichever is the case, the time is well spent, because the file is how many different people will judge you for the next year. The judgment they make will determine whether you stay at your current institution and continue to advance professionally or must look for another position under less than desirable conditions.

The Personal Statement

Most universities and colleges require tenure candidates to include a personal statement in their files. Many places impose a mandatory limit on personal statement length. At some colleges, the limit is short (1 to 2 pages), while at others the limit is longer (5 to 10 pages). If there are no written rules on the length of the personal statement, find out the informal norms. A one-page statement at a college where five is typical makes the candidate appear cocky, unconcerned, or dumb. None of these characteristics are the image to convey in your tenure decision year. A 10-page statement if two is the norm may imply that you are too worried and unsure of yourself, long-winded, or pompous.

Think about your statement before you write. This is your opportunity to make your own case and to justify why you should be tenured and promoted. This in not the place to be modest. Write about your achievements and "toot your own horn," but in a subtle fashion. For example, do not say that you are the best researcher of all time, but do indicate the importance of your last three papers. If several well-known scholars have written asking for further details about the new scale reported in one of your articles, mention this as you discuss your future plans for this line of research.

At most universities, one important aspect of the personal statement is including goals for the future and demonstrating that you have a research agenda beyond achieving tenure. Some details about future plans should be included in your discussion of research. If possible, locate your future work (and your past work) within a larger body of work in the subfield. Depending on the university or college, goals for the future may also be expected in teaching, service, and total professional development. Table 4.3 lists some of the major elements often included in a personal statement, but remember to find out the specific rules at your institution and follow those, adapting these general suggestions to the specifics of your institution.

Along with the external reviews, the personal statement may be very important for evaluation by oversight committees and administrators. This statement gives a quick sense of whether you know who you are and where you are going in your career. An oversight committee member is more likely to read a four-page statement carefully than to read your last three articles. The same is true for a dean or provost. Just as the overall file provides the overall total impression of the candidate, the personal statement is the single quickest impression you provide. Moreover, this statement, along with your curriculum vita, is often provided to the outside reviewers, along with selected papers. The statement may help to influence a positive evaluation by the outside reviewer by providing a coherent organizing theme for your work. The

Table 4.3 Items Often Included in Personal Statement

Research: Generally the most critical part and required by most institutions.
Review your past accomplishments.
Place your research into a unified framework.
Place your work within the discipline and subfields.
List goals for the future that build on your past research, including a mention of current projects under way.
Teaching: Often not required; still may help to mention in a brief paragraph.
Include some brief statement of goals to continue to improve teaching.
If interested in trying innovative teaching methods, mention that goals are to work with more advanced students or whatever is appropriate to your circumstance.
Service: Often not required, but might mention briefly.
List any major interests or goals.
Often a goal at the stage of making tenure is to gain more visibility in national professional and disciplinary associations through holding offices, etc.
Summary: Summarize with an integrative statement of goals for total professional development.

---

weaker the candidate's case, the more important the personal statement. Also, if you have been criticized for doing scattered research or not having a major thrust, the statement is your opportunity to demonstrate to others the connections in your research. Lastly, have people outside your university or your department or close junior colleagues read the statement and critique it. It is as important to receive critical comments on the statement as it is on the next article you send out.

External Reviewers

At many universities and colleges, one of the most critical portions of the tenure process is provided by letters from external reviewers evaluating the tenure candidate's scholarly and service productivity. Universities vary widely on how these letters are obtained. Formally, most universities have two sets of reviewers. One set is named by the candidate. A second set is selected by the department chair or the tenured faculty.

Informally, colleges differ. Most departments ask for more names from the tenure candidate than they will actually use. In some departments, the chair will unofficially talk to the candidate about reviewer selection by asking such questions as "Do you have any problem with Green?" or "Have you talked much about your work with Brown at meetings?" In other departments, such informal probing would be considered dishonest and inappropriate. Some departments do develop an independent list of reviewers other than those provided by the candidate, while the most rigorous of departments will not ask the candidates for names at all but simply have the chair or senior faculty choose the external referees.

How do you choose the list of names to serve as external reviewers? Who do you decide to list and not list? Throughout your career, it is helpful to develop a colleague network at other institutions. Junior faculty may do this through personal contact at professional meetings, through serving on panels with faculty from other colleges, through collaborating and publishing with faculty from elsewhere, and through a less formal exchange of manuscripts and scholarly ideas. It is important to develop this colleague network throughout the pretenure period. It aids in developing ideas, in having references for other jobs, and in having reliable colleagues willing to serve as external reviewers at tenure time. Some professional societies have set up formal mentoring programs to help young scholars network with senior researchers and learn how to develop a colleague network. If your field does not have this option available, begin to develop a network yourself. Ask the discussant of a session in which you presented a paper if he or she would be willing to read additional papers of yours. If you have made friends with several other junior people in your area who have their degrees from different institutions than you, help one another out at meetings by mutual introductions to your advisers. Going to meetings is very helpful in developing a colleague network, because

Table 4.4 Criteria to Select Referees for Outside Letters

Pick people at equivalent peer or better institutions, but be sure they understand the norms of your kind of institution.

Use no more than one referee from your doctoral institution.

Use only one person from a group with which you have written articles (preferably the most senior person).

Referees should be at a higher rank than you.

Include full professors along with associate professors.

Contact people in advance before putting their name on your list.

Do not include someone who indicates they are too busy or unfamiliar with your work.

---

senior people are more likely to respond later to someone they have already met and talked to than to a letter from an unknown asking for a review of a new manuscript. Sometimes, however, a polite letter requesting a review of a paper or comments on an idea will work, especially if you know it relates to the person's current work or builds on their past published work (perhaps followed up by a phone call).

Generally, outside referees should be at a higher academic rank than the candidate and preferably at equivalently or more prestigious colleges and universities. If a reviewer is well known as the best expert in a subfield, even at a less prestigious university, he or she may be an excellent referee but it is useful to inform the chair of the department about the person's prominence so they can include such facts in their own letter. If you are being promoted to associate professor, it is reasonable to have both full and associate professors as reviewers, although to have no full professors write external letters would be regarded as a sign of weakness at many universities. (See Table 4.4.)

Can the referees be people with close contact with the candidate? Usually no more than one referee from your doctoral-granting institution should be used, because these people are viewed as having a vested interest in the achievements of former doctoral students. Similarly, if you have a group of colleagues with whom you publish often, a letter from one person in the group (probably the most senior group member) is appropriate, but you should not have all letters from that group.

Outside references should be from appropriate universities. Most universities have a sense of peer institutions, places similar to themselves or slightly better. You want your references to be from places of similar or better quality. To list, however, only the best people from the best places can be a dangerous strategy. Often one question addressed to the reviewer is whether the candidate would obtain tenure at the reviewer's own institution. If standards for tenure at that university exceed those of your own, the interpretation from the outside reviewer may be unclear.

Statements such as "Although the candidate would not obtain tenure here, the record appears more appropriate for your level of institution" are not that helpful and may be harmful to the candidate's chances. Even more harmful is the unqualified statement, such as "This candidate's rate of scholarly productivity is only half that of recent candidates in this department." Reviewers from peer institutions are more likely to be able to judge appropriately and have a sense of reasonable levels of expectations. If you are at a small college, others in similar settings are probably appropriate references, along with one or two well-known people at the more research-oriented places, if they are appropriate, given the nature of your type of research.

Should you contact people in advance before including their names as references? A useful approach in the year and summer before preparation of the file is to contact those whose names you plan to submit. Ask them if they are agreeable or would like to examine some of your work before deciding to be an external reviewer.

Often people may remove themselves from the list by being on sabbatical or by implying that others would be better choices. Do not include on your list those who have declined. They may be negative toward you and your work. Their reluctance to participate on other grounds is simply a face-saving excuse for you not to include them. They may also be legitimately too busy and never write the much needed letter. In either case, the inclusion of such a person will not help.

At times, a good strategy is to contact more people than the number required for your list. Then decide which people your unit will be unlikely to think of and include some of those people on your list. By leaving off some more obvious choices who you feel will be positive about your candidacy, you may increase the chances that your chair or department will contact that person. If there is someone in the field who you believe is unfairly negative about you or a particular aspect of your work, then ask your department chair if you can request that this person *not* be included as a reference.

A Year of Waiting

Waiting is often difficult and tense. Because many universities require a file to be submitted to the department in September but do not inform the candidate of the decision until April, this can be a long year. It may not be a bad strategy to apply to selected positions at other institutions—for your own mental health. It is always nice to know that you have options other than unemployment, especially if you feel less confident about a positive outcome. Do not panic or worry too much, however. A candidate will usually have an additional year of employment at the same university after a denial of tenure, during which time he or she can seek employment in a different setting.

Finally, you may try to find out whether it is appropriate to ask where things are, how your case is progressing, and whether you will receive any information during the year. Probably the better you know and get along with the chair, the more likely you will be to hear some informal sense of progression, unless your university has strong formal rules against any information being given to the candidate.

Being Denied Tenure

For some people, the final result will be an unhappy decision. If denied tenure, what should you do? First, examine your own record and what has happened in the institution. Decide if you want to appeal. Do not assume you will start with a court suit. You must follow and exhaust your own institution's rules for internal appeal before you can file a suit in court. Rules vary at each institution, but typically you may have only a few days in which to decide whether to begin an appeal. Almost every academic institution today has spelled out policies as to how to handle grievances and denials of tenure. You must find out the process at your own institution and follow it carefully. Failure to follow the rules can have a request for a review denied on procedural grounds, just as in a court case.

Should you appeal? Can you obtain help on an appeal? If your campus is unionized, talk to the officials from the union. They will typically provide help and give you good advice on the strength of your appeal. If it is not strong and you have made friends with senior faculty members outside your department (and perhaps outside your college), talk to them. You may wish to obtain legal advice. Unless there is a union to provide legal aid, this can be expensive. If you do contact a lawyer, be sure he or she has some experience in academic suits. The legal issues and rules differ from other types of labor or general law. In addition to the financial costs of an appeal, the process drains time and energy. You should consult with friends and colleagues from other institutions about how likely you are to win an appeal. Also, how good or bad is the job market? How tied are you through a spouse's job or other

Table 4.5 Revoking Tenure

Reasons for revoking tenure:
    moral turpitude
    conviction of criminal conduct
    academic fraud, including
        plagiarism
        falsification of academic credentials
        falsification of research data and results
        falsification of research and work record
    proven malfeasance or failure to perform contractual duties, including
        regularly missing scheduled classes with no justification
        appearing in class drunk
        appearing in class under the influence of drugs
    financial exigencies
    shifting institutional priorities resulting in the abolition of the tenure
    unit

---

connections to remaining in the same geographic area? If you have a good record and are geographically mobile, finding a new tenure-track position may be a better alternative than exhausting money, time, and energy on an appeal.

Revoking Tenure

Tenure normally means lifetime job security. Few other occupations in the United States offer the prospect of guaranteed lifetime employment. Of course, the employment guarantee of tenure is not absolute. Tenure may be revoked for several reasons. (See Table 4.5.)

Most colleges have provisions that allow "moral turpitude" to be used as a rationale for dismissing a tenured faculty member. What "moral turpitude" means is not always clear, and proving it is very difficult. In some instances, substantiated sexual harassment of students has constituted proof and tenure has been revoked.

Conviction of criminal conduct in an established court of law is also grounds for firing tenured faculty. Convictions may include theft of institutional property, embezzlement of funds, or even drug-related charges.

Academic fraud, including plagiarism of scholarly work, falsification of academic credentials and professional record including publications, and falsification of research results may also result in dismissal of tenured faculty. These grounds are infrequently applied, however, because proving academic fraud especially in research requires professional self-regulation. University and college professors have proven no more willing or skilled at the unpleasant and onerous task of publicly charging their colleagues of inappropriate and unacceptable conduct than have other ostensibly self-regulating professions, including medicine and law.

Proven malfeasance or failure to perform basic contractual duties may result in the dismissal of tenured faculty. Usually this means the professor routinely fails to show up for regularly scheduled classes without a reasonable excuse or frequently shows up visibly drunk or under the influence of drugs.

Financial exigencies may result in the dismissal of tenured faculty. Usually, universities and colleges facing financial difficulties engage in bone-cutting reductions in other functions and personnel before laying off tenured professors. When financial difficulties first arise, support activities will be curtailed and capital projects will be deferred. If hard times persist, building maintenance will be delayed, and administrative, janitorial, and campus police personnel may be laid off before professors are touched. When faculty must be reduced because of financial stress, untenured faculty members will be dismissed first. Only as a last resort are tenured members laid off.

Shifting institutional priorities constitute yet another ground for dismissing tenured faculty members, but this rationale is rarely used. On occasion, a university or college may decide it no longer needs nor can afford an entire academic department or discipline. All tenured faculty within the affected department may be fired and the department may be disbanded.

The fraction of departments to which this has occurred, however, is minuscule.

The AAUP carefully monitors decisions to fire tenured faculty as well as tenure processes. It publishes a censure list of colleges found to violate AAUP rules about granting tenure and honoring tenure protection. Faculty members who feel their tenure protection has been unfairly violated and who have exhausted internal appeals processes may also sue their former employers. Few words strike more fear into university administrators than the dreaded "lawsuit." Filing civil suit, however, does not guarantee judicial success to dismissed tenured professors guilty of wrongdoing or those laid off because of financial distress.

5 | Meeting the Research Criterion

The scholarship or research criterion for tenure is an important one. In theory, the research criterion often holds the same weight in the tenure decision, and the three criteria are stated to be equal. In reality, the scholarship criterion may be informally viewed as more important than the other two criteria of teaching and service, especially at major research universities. In our observations, more tenure candidates are denied tenure because of inadequate scholarship than because of failure to meet the other two criteria. In recent decades, expectations for scholarship have been rising, not just at research universities, but also at other smaller, less comprehensive universities and colleges. "Publish or perish" is not just an idle threat!

In scientific fields as well as in some applied social sciences, research also involves getting grants. Large grant getters are eminently more tenurable than those with limited or no success at bringing grant funds into the institution. Just as greater prestige is attached to peer-reviewed publications, university tenure norms place greater prestige on nationally competitive peer-reviewed grants. A track record in getting grants alone, however, is insufficient to meet the research criterion. Grants must result in research that ends up in peer-reviewed publications in journals. Given the lead time in getting competitive grants, as well as the often lengthy process in getting publications accepted in peer-reviewed journals, tenure candidates have little time to lose while their tenure clock is ticking.

Despite the expectations that tenure candidates will have developed a suitable scholarly record supported by a publication record that includes some peer-reviewed work, graduate students in the course of their Ph.D. work are rarely taught how to publish. At research-oriented universities where many faculty members publish, information on how to publish may be more readily available than at less research-oriented universities where only a few faculty members are actively publishing. Even at research-oriented universities, however, professors training Ph.D.s with aspirations of an academic career may feel compelled to establish a "public face" that covers up the more harrowing and trying aspects of the publishing process, as well as the numerous rejections and revisions that it may entail. To understand these as a graduate student, you must win the confidence of a faculty member who becomes a true mentor, sharing both the joys of victory and the agony of defeat. In most Ph.D. training departments, how to survive the publishing process is currently taught through voluntary apprenticeships if at all.

If you are still in graduate school, it is not too early to begin thinking about publishing and even trying to do so. If you have a strong and active faculty adviser or promoter, you might express your desire to begin publishing and ask for advice. The faculty may help you revise one of your better seminar papers for this purpose. Some faculty members have grants or research projects themselves and are willing to include capable Ph.D. students on these projects. Further, if you work closely with your dissertation adviser, you may copublish one or more articles from your dissertation with your adviser.

In any of these settings, this is your first introduction to the reality that who gets credit for research in academics is a sensitive matter. You may have a generous adviser who is willing to provide you large amounts of assistance, support, and guidance with no credit. But many faculty members, under pressure to publish themselves, want to be included as coauthors on the publications of graduate students with whom they work. Indeed, the prospect of your adviser getting additional publications is a carrot you can use as a graduate student to encourage your adviser to help you and to take an interest in your work. If you did not start publishing in graduate school, when you land your first tenure-track job, you must learn how to do it and begin to do so. To delay until you are comfortable in your new job and have worked out other aspects of your life, teaching, and dealing with new colleagues is to risk not having enough time to compile an acceptable publication record before your tenure clock runs out. When your colleagues evaluate your record later to see if it meets the scholarship criterion, many aspects of publishing are not clear-cut and require judgment calls: whether your research is of sufficiently high quality, who did how much on coauthored works, and so on. But whether you published is unambiguous and clear. So begin!

Why Publish?

Is publishing the part of your job as a professor that you dread? Perhaps you have no specific idea for how to go about establishing an appropriate and reasonable research agenda and then implementing it. Perhaps you have already received your first rejection and found it brutal and shattering to your self-confidence. You may wonder, given the difficulties and frustrations associated with publishing, why do it? Many people, in fact, do not. Some quit publishing once they have acquired tenure, remaining associate professors in research-oriented institutions for the duration of their career or else rising to professor rank on the basis of service or administrative contributions in institutions where research is emphasized less. Others never seriously start to do research, eventually leaving academics entirely, sometimes after two or three stints at different universities or colleges where failing to publish resulted in termination. Others start at community colleges or teaching-oriented colleges where publishing is not expected—yet. But if you have angst over the prospect of sending out your best ideas and work for total strangers to anonymously tear apart in the peer-review process, then remember that publishing is an exhilarating as well as agonizing process. It can be uplifting as well as bruising. Nor are research and publishing as isolating as they once were in many fields, especially the physical, biological, and social sciences. The traditional myth of academic publishing depicts the ivory-towered scholar, sheltered from the helter skelter and hubbub of the ordinary world, allowed to contemplate in reflective solitude and leisure. The reality of publishing is often frantic, frenzied, and frustrating, as prospective authors rush to meet deadlines for grant applications, data entry, preliminary reports, drafts, revisions, copy editing, and page-proof corrections. The real world of team research requires coordination with collaborators, supervising assistants, prodding colleagues, massaging egos, refereeing substantive and personality conflicts, and creating a just distribution of rewards. Even if you are in fields such as humanities and literature where solitary research is the norm, presenting your findings through scholarly papers at meetings can be a form of social and intellectual pleasure, as well as providing contact with important people in your field.

Publishing: Essential to an Academic Career

Most universities and colleges have a scholarship tenure requirement. Publishing, especially in outlets where work is peer-reviewed, is the accepted approach for demonstrating that you have fulfilled this criterion. National data showing that of the total professoriate, only a small portion are actively publishing do not depict the reality you confront in your efforts to get tenure. These data capture the inertia and low turnover in the academy resulting from a heavily tenured total faculty. Many nonpublishing faculty members are already tenured; if confronted with a current tenure decision on their careers, they would be denied. The relevant data base for you as a new Ph.D. is much smaller: the records of faculty members recently promoted and tenured in your own institution and department.

If you decide that you do not want to publish and seek out a college that does not require publishing to get tenure, you do so at your own risk. In the past, increases in expectations for research have occurred at four-year state colleges as well as private colleges that previously required little or no publication. Requirements for publication at large universities, especially flagship state universities, have also increased as these institutions vie for a greater share of research dollars to impress state legislators. Private universities, often confronting fiscal austerity, have also been forced to rely more heavily on research dollars. These trends have increased pressure on faculty members to publish and become professionally visible in order to attract grant funding.

In most universities and colleges, new attention to teaching has not reduced significantly the expectations for publication and research that tenure candidates confront. The recent renewed emphasis on quality teaching, especially at the undergraduate level, has increased total expectations on new Ph.D.s rather than reallocated emphasis among criteria for junior faculty academic success. Research and publishing are not valued less just because teaching is valued more. Hard-pressed university administrators, caught by parental and student resistance to increased tuition, rising costs, and strapped budgets, are always searching for ways to get more from constant or shrinking resources. Rising rather than off-setting expectations on faculty are a natural consequence of tight budgets. Increased expectations for publishing are a key part of those increases.

Publishing: Informs and Improves Teaching

Research and publishing are often depicted as inversely related to quality teaching, when the relationship between the two is more commonly positive. The knowledge and perspective you acquire from your research and literature searches related to publishing can improve your teaching and help you meet the teaching criterion. This is especially true if you teach graduate seminars at a major research university, but it also applies in other settings. The great teacher who never writes or researches is rapidly becoming a myth. More typically, good teachers continually think about, read about, and probe questions in their field. The process of publishing and responding to peer reviews forces this examination and currentness and helps them stay on top of their fields. Without the structured incentive generated by publishing to stay current, you may be tempted to rely on dog-eared notes, just like some professors you once had and probably did not like.

What informs and improves teaching may vary by level of instruction. Introductory texts and survey books, while not traditional research, represent syntheses of the current state of knowledge in a broad area. Researching and writing these volumes will force you constantly to survey relevant literature and events to incorporate into the next text edition. Failure to do so loses sales and lowers the knowledge base for lectures. Before your tenure decision, however, you should determine the attitude of your departmental colleagues toward textbooks before devoting much time to writing one. In some universities, texts are viewed as evidence supporting the teaching criterion, not the scholarship criterion. In some departments in major research universities, authoring texts is even regarded as a negative, reflecting misplaced time and detracting from a more serious research agenda. If you have a real penchant for writing texts and are in such a department, you can do so after tenure. In teaching-oriented departments, however, authoring a well-regarded text is viewed as evidence of scholarship. It is important to find out the norms in your department before launching into writing one before tenure. If in doubt, do not write one until you have gotten tenure. Pursue shorter, more quickly completed projects instead. Introductory courses are not the only areas of teaching that are improved by publishing activities. Upper-division undergraduate and graduate courses are improved when you are conducting research in the area. Special topics books, original manuscripts, and journal articles all contribute to your knowledge of ongoing controversies. In graduate seminars, using the methodological techniques and approaches in current journal articles in your own research helps you better explain the utility and limitations of those techniques under various conditions.

Mature students are increasing in numbers and in the proportion they constitute of total student enrollment in institutions of higher education. The proportion of traditional students between ages 18 and 22 is shrinking. Further, the number of students pursuing second, third, and fourth graduate degrees is increasing. As the student body matures, the quality and content of teaching changes, as well as what is needed to command the respect of older students. Students become more demanding, critical, and willing to challenge poor teaching. Publications and research command the respect of mature students who recognize that you have produced relevant knowledge in the field. Publications also ensure that you keep current and are closer to the cutting edge. The current familiarity with relevant professional literature and approaches that publishing requires provides this additional specialized knowledge to the classroom that more mature students want.

The Scalpel, Shotgun, and Double-Helix Publishing Models

Professors vary greatly in their approaches to publishing. Rather than a single model of success, there are at least three different models. Which to use depends on your intellectual talents, skills, and proclivities, as well as on the expectations of your department.

If you use the scalpel model to develop a publishing record for tenure and beyond, you select a narrow area in which to concentrate and strive to become one of a handful of national experts in this area. One of your primary goals is to influence other professionals who also publish in the narrow area. If you succeed in doing so, you can readily solicit external letters from scholars in the same field who know your work well for tenure. Although scalpel scholars may know about and even occasionally publish in a subfield closely related to their major specialization, when there are trade-offs between depth and breadth, scalpel scholars opt for penetrating depth. Less successful scalpel scholars may study the trivial because the data are readily available or because they cannot think of anything else to do. More successful scalpel scholars significantly advance major subfields; some even found major subfields.

In the shotgun model of publishing, you research and write on a broad array of topics and in many subfields. Some shotgun scholars are even interdisciplinary, crossing major academic disciplinary boundaries to conduct research in several. Shotgun scholars usually publish a lot and compile very lengthy vitae. If you use this approach to meet the tenure research criterion, you will likely have enough publications, although you may be criticized for their quality, as well as for being scattered and lacking focus.

Across a career, shotgun scholars may develop substantial knowledge in some subspecialties. When trade-offs occur between depth and breadth, however, shotgun scholars opt for sweeping panoramic breadth. Less successful shotgun scholars may never tie together into a coherent whole the various pieces of their seemingly disparate interests. More successful shotgun scholars are able to integrate and synthesize knowledge from various fields.

In the double-helix model of research and publishing, a scholar's career becomes a series of shifts back and forth between the academic world and the real world of politics and policy making. Thus you pursue two intertwining tracks simultaneously, much as the genetic strands of the DNA molecule intertwine in a double-helix formation. Each shift and twist feeds not only future progress on the current track but also on the intertwining track.

Under the double-helix approach, you use an initial scholarly publication to achieve press and public attention, proving adept at communicating with broader audiences as well as with professional ones. The public attention you receive and your role in real-world events then increase academic attention and opportunities, which in turn help fuel future forays into the public arena.

No publishing approach is inherently superior to the others. Plainly, any one of the three may lead to personal, individual success. The choice of which model to use may be almost subconscious and inadvertent, resulting from an interaction of mental proclivities and opportunities. One problem concerning these models, however, is that sometimes people who employ one model may be less tolerant of or threatened by scholars using an alternative model. You should watch out for these possible conflicts and try to avoid becoming a casualty of any career-approach conflict. Conflict with senior and other colleagues before your tenure decision undercuts your efforts to build a positive coalition on your behalf.

Senior scalpel scholars may view junior shotgun scholars as too scattered, too spread out, and overcommitted. Because scalpel scholars do not feel comfortable themselves pursuing multiple avenues of inquiry simultaneously, they may question why and how anyone else could competently engage in such pursuit. In tense situations, this amazed bewilderment may veer into hostility.

Senior shotgun scholars may not be hostile to junior scalpel scholars, but they may find them boring and simply ignore them. Junior scalpel scholars neither know as much nor have produced as much as senior scalpel scholars, who may have won the begrudging respect of senior shotgun scholars. Thus, senior shotgun scholars may exhibit indifference to and ignorance of the accomplishments of junior scalpel scholars, instead of positive support. Everybody may be envious of or hostile to budding double-helix scholars. An unmeasured and possibly unknowable proportion of senior scholars never had, do not currently have, and never will have media skills. These senior scholars may think junior double-helix scholars are too slick, too upstart, and not sufficiently academic. The best strategy is to develop a healthy appreciation for the publishing models used by your colleagues while encouraging them to appreciate the advantages of your own.

Should You Collaborate in Research and With Whom?

Should you collaborate? In general, the more scientific the field, the more collaborative the research and writing; the less scientific the field, the greater the expectations that professors will conduct research and writing on their own. The physical, biological, and health sciences have emphasized collaborative research, although some exceptions do occur, such as theoretical physics. The humanities have emphasized solitary research. Social sciences have fallen in the middle rather than either extreme, because both collaborative and solitary models are allowed. Subtly and slowly, however, the balance is shifting toward collaborative research. Two factors are contributing to this shift in the social sciences.

❶ Most social sciences are not as grant-dependent as the physical, biological, and health sciences, where failure to become part of grant-getting research teams results in professional isolation and failure. The role of grants is rising, however, as theory testing of social theories requires larger data bases, more surveys, painstaking data collection, and other costly activities. And grants typically require collaboration and research teams.

❷ Expectations about publishing volume have been rising, and people who publish together largely publish more than people who publish alone.

In the humanities and arts, collaboration may still have a negative connotation. If you are in such a specialty, you should find out the norms in your department. If all of your publications are with other people, especially people from your former graduate school, you may be seen as being unable to start an independent research agenda. It is important to try to be first author on at least some of your jointly authored publications. Some observers place great importance on the order in which the names of authors are listed, attributing the value of the contribution to the project by the place in ordering. Finding good collaborators is very important. The more specialized your interests are, the more difficult the search for research collaborators becomes. When possible, you should write with four types of people: friends, people who can help you, people who complement your weaknesses, and those who are better than you. Friends make good collaborators because research and writing are very intimate activities. If you have a choice between working with someone who will help your career and someone who will have no long-term positive impact on it beyond the immediate project, pick the former. In essence, seek out mentors who will help guide your decisions in important, crucial, formative pretenure years and who will become champions for you.

The robust scholar who does it all is a very rare find. Most scholars have strengths and weaknesses. Self-aware new Ph.D.s will ideally find collaborators whose strengths complement their own weaknesses. Some typical "pairs" of complementary skills involved in research and publication include writing drafts versus finished papers, excelling at abstract ideas versus factual details, and comfort with words versus numbers.

Academics is not unlike tennis or any other sport: The way to improve is to play with people who are better than you.

Table 5.1 Developing Your Publication Record

Publish from your dissertation.
When in doubt, publish articles instead of books before tenure.
Use conferences as a writing deadline and for networking.
Target articles for a variety of journals.
Treat writing as a regular part of your job.
Avoid administrative and other distractions.
Develop a tough ego to be able to handle negative reviews.
Assist editors and reviewers in seeing your revisions and accommodate their criticisms.
Find out the research standards for your department, even if they are not stated explicitly.
Ask senior colleagues their expectations.
Examine the records of recently tenured faculty.
Pay attention to criticisms in your annual reviews.
Keep good records and copies of all your published and unpublished research.
Demonstrate a coherent, ongoing research agenda.

Playing with betters as opposed to inferiors requires a strong ego that is not threatened by the fact that others are better. But if your ego can take the comparison, your research skills and output will improve. Collaborators may be better because they are more knowledgeable, have more connections, have more skills, are smarter, or are more energetic.

Developing Your Publication Record

Here are more tips about how to develop your publication record for tenure (see Table 5.1):

Publish from your dissertation. It is an unusual Ph.D. student who, upon successful completion of his or her dissertation, does not want to throw up at the mere mention of any single word included in the dissertation title, much less the whole title. Try to resist this impulse, take an adequate dose of antacid, and continue working with the dissertation. Envision getting publications out of it as just another stage in the whole dissertation defense.

Dissertations that hang together should be revised for possible publication with a university or specialty press. Other dissertations may be more amenable to spinning out one or more discrete articles. By all means, however, *do not* send the dissertation out unrevised, because everyone will recognize it precisely for what it is: a tortuously written, overly pedantic, unrevised dissertation. Solicit the help of senior scholars who might help your career to get ideas about revisions and publication outlets.

When in doubt, gravitate toward articles over books until after tenure or after publishing enough articles to reasonably ensure tenure. Major books can have major impact and secure significant recognition, but you probably cannot produce one before your tenure clock runs out. Your probability of producing a series of discrete, competently researched and written articles is much greater. With articles, the rejection of one does not necessarily undermine the prospects of another. A book, by contrast, may take a year or two of effort, during which you may be doing little else.

Publication of a book important to your tenure record may be delayed for a variety of reasons, some beyond your control. Considerable turmoil and mergers among publishers of college books may cause the author to go through several editors or publishing houses in a short time. In many departments, textbooks are not regarded as research publications. Specialized books that can be used in class may fall into a gray area.

Once in print, your book may be unfavorably reviewed, especially if it focuses on controversial issues. By contrast, reviews of articles occur before they are published and are not themselves published. Finally, peer-reviewed publications are respected everywhere and are absolutely essential in many universities. If you succeed in getting tenure, then many working years remain to tackle longer, book-length projects.

Use conferences as a writing deadline as well as an opportunity for professional networking. You should strive to present papers at conferences, because fear of showing up at the conference and being castigated by the chair and discussant for having no paper is a powerful motivator. Conferences create real deadlines that make sleep less important than writing. Further, comments from a good discussant alert you to likely criticisms when the article is sent out for publication and may save one or more rounds of reviews. Similarly, comments from off-the-wall discussants may also alert you to likely publication-review criticisms and also save one round of reviews.

Solid legitimate criticisms should be addressed in revisions, and other criticisms might be anticipated and countered. Feedback from conferences as well as the contacts established there are particularly important if you are employed in a department where either not many other people publish or no one is there who has the expertise to thoughtfully read your work.

Target articles for a variety of journals. Any particular editor or journal may be biased against your scholarly approach, so trying a variety of journals may be useful. Because rejection rates at prestigious journals are usually higher than others, a mixture of journals increases the overall probability of success. New journals provide a good outlet for junior scholars, because new journals often do not have a backlog of old manuscripts that delay publication once an article is accepted or that cause an editor to automatically reject an article in tough judgment calls.

Treat writing as a regular part of your job. You may choose between two different approaches to writing. One is the "student" model; the other is the "bureaucratic employee" model. Under the student model, you delay and procrastinate until a deadline approaches, then drop all other activities, and bury yourself in the task of producing the analysis and article or paper needed to meet a deadline. This "cramming" model resembles a student cramming the night or day before a major exam.

The cramming model, while quite effective at times, has several problems. First, it assumes that waiting until the last minute will not engender difficulties in data analysis, computer runs, writing, and other stages of production. Second, the older you get, the harder it gets to cram.

By contrast, the bureaucratic employee model implies that you treat writing and research as a regular part of the job of being a faculty member, setting aside a fixed amount of time in a week to pursue these activities. The bureaucratic model emphasizes regularity of effort rather than the motivation of impending deadlines. This model is easier to maintain as your career matures. A mixture of models early in your career might be beneficial, but at some time it is beneficial to adopt the bureaucratic model at least in parallel with, if not to the exclusion of, the student model.

Avoid administrative and other distractions. A few rare talented individuals can do their own jobs and those of five or six others. But most cannot, including most junior scholars. Just as the primary job of a senior graduate student is to write a dissertation, your primary job as an untenured junior scholar is to produce enough publications to get tenure. Being the best teacher in the world and failing to publish enough to get tenure will cause the loss of the opportunity to be a teacher at all. Running major university committees and activities while still untenured at the expense of sufficient attention to your research and scholarship will also remove future opportunities to serve on university committees.

Benign departments try to protect you from overcommitments in administration and committee work. Less benign departments may assign you to numerous committees and administrative tasks to get maximal output for the institution from you in your pretenure years, deny you tenure for not producing research and scholarship because of your other assignments, and then recruit new junior faculty members to fill your place. Be street smart and try to avoid this trap, while still demonstrating some commitment to service.

Develop a tough ego to be able to handle negative reviews. Publishing in a peer-review process is not for the fainthearted. Rarely is an article accepted outright. Even accepted articles often must often undergo revisions. You will hear both warranted and unwarranted criticism. Be aware that the peer-review process is generally heavily biased against interdisciplinary issues and approaches and toward the status quo orthodoxy and paradigm. If your research does not fit this model, you should "cover" yourself before tenure by publishing at least some more traditional pieces.

Because the peer-review process is blind, reviewers are not accountable directly to authors, only to editors. Although good editors weed out vitriolic reviewers who make nonhelpful and at times sarcastic and even nasty comments, some inappropriately vicious reviews may slip through. Move on to something else, and when your emotions have cooled come back to the reviews.

Even more hurtful are critical reviews that have legitimate complaints, precisely because they are on target and therefore cannot be dismissed lightly. A good strategy when an editor returns a verdict is to read an initial decision, quickly read critical reviews, and then set them aside for a week or so while working on other things. This brief hiatus gives you a week or so to accommodate the emotional reality of having to revise the piece on which you have long labored, in some instances, having to make fundamental changes. After a week or two, reread the reviews carefully and seriously to develop a strategy and schedule for making specific changes.

Assist editors and reviewers to see how your revised manuscript has accommodated their concerns. Even if a junior scholar does not agree with all criticisms received in the peer-review process, it is a good idea to attempt to accommodate as many criticisms as possible when making revisions. Despite a sometimes powerful emotional reaction to criticisms, fights with editors and reviewers rarely pay off. When accommodation is not possible, specify why.

When returning an article that has been accepted with revisions or resubmitting an article when the decision was to revise and resubmit, specify in a cover letter to the editor all the changes made and how each reviewer criticism the editor thought significant was addressed. Again, if reviewer-specified changes are not possible, indicate to the editor why.

Know when to stop writing. Sometimes you have invested so much of yourself into a paper that it is hard to let go. More than anyone else, you are aware of how additional work could improve any particular piece. But papers are somewhat like children. After a certain point, one has to send them out into the world to let them stand or fall on their own. A good paper that gets published and lets you move on to the next article or study is better than the unpublished masterpiece that stays on your shelf.

When in doubt, write. A common saying is that if you have to ask the price, you aren't rich enough. The publishing parallel is that if you have to ask if you have now published enough to get tenure, then you have not. Of course, standards for how much is enough to meet the research criterion change across time and vary across departments and universities.

Find out the standards your department uses. Many times you will not be directly told how much to publish. However, it is your responsibility to find out what your department's standards are. Do this by talking with senior department colleagues and get their assessments of what is expected to meet the research criterion. Also examine the records of people who have received tenure in the past few years. Pay attention to your annual evaluations and be sensitive to any feedback about the adequacy of your publishing record that these reviews provide.

Some departments stress peer-review journals more than others. Departments that highly value prestigious peer-review articles may even publish a list of acceptable journals and expect tenure candidates to have an adequate number of articles in those journals. If you are in such a department, you must attempt to have a minimum number of articles in journals on the list. Other departments are more flexible and value a wider variety of journals. When you submit your tenure file, you may be required to separate peer-reviewed from nonpeer-reviewed publications. Pay attention to how many peer-reviewed articles you have.

Keep good records and copies of all your published and unpublished research. Good record keeping is important in building a tenure file. Keep copies of all of your conference papers and, obviously, your publications. You will likely be asked to include reprints of your journal articles in your tenure file, and you may be asked to include conference papers as well. Update the publications on your vita regularly, giving proper citations for articles and other research when it appears in print.

Demonstrate a coherent ongoing research agenda. When reviewing your tenure file, most colleagues will want to see evidence that you have a coherent ongoing research agenda. If you are a scalpel scholar, the coherence will be more readily obvious than if you are a shotgun scholar. If you have published in a variety of areas, take pains in your personal statement to show the common themes in your research, pointing to articles and papers that fit into each theme or subarea. Do not appear to be too scattered. Try to be first author on at least some coauthored publications to circumvent criticism that you are not capable of initiating and structuring projects. If you have gaps in your record because of personal circumstances or other factors, mention why the gaps appear but do not dwell on the explanations or you will appear to be whining. Most important, colleagues and administrators will want evidence that you will continue to publish and conduct research after you receive tenure. Point out ongoing research projects and talk about future research and publishing goals.

No one cares as much about your articles or your career as you do. When tenure decisions are being made, ignorance about the standards is not bliss; nor is ignorance usually an acceptable excuse for not having met them. If this pressure to publish seems stressful, ponder carefully the career alternatives: surviving in a dog-eat-dog corporate world with 80-hour workweeks and little or no autonomy; selling insurance on commission; teaching five hours every single day and grading papers a hundred hours each night at a local high school—if you are willing to go back and spend a year getting a teaching certificate; and so forth. So how bad can exploring and writing on a topic of your own choosing and of intense interest to you be? Academics is like the United States: More people want to get in than get out. The reason is not hard to discern: In addition to the job security, autonomy, freedom, and flexibility, few other jobs offer the potential for self-esteem, self-actualization, and societal impact as do research and scholarship on important topics.

6 | Meeting the Teaching Criterion

After decades of placing greater emphasis on research and publishing than on teaching, most universities and colleges in recent years have devoted renewed attention to teaching, especially at the undergraduate level. Indeed, in some colleges and universities, teaching is stressed over research or service. The new focus on teaching may be reinforced by requirements in some institutions that merit pay be linked to teaching excellence and constitute as much as one half or more of the basis for merit raises. In other academic settings, teaching may be a smaller component in appraising overall performance, but poor teaching may be used to deny tenure.

If you are just beginning your academic career on a tenure-track job, teaching may seem exhausting and overwhelming. Developing several new courses simultaneously is a lot of work! Lecture notes and seminar preparation are time-consuming, especially at first. But given the renewed emphasis on quality teaching, developing good teaching skills is important for meeting your tenure criterion. In smaller liberal arts and teaching-oriented colleges, your job and career depend on these skills above all else.

Teaching well is a subjective art, but it is also a skill that can be improved on if not perfected. All teachers have moments of great frustration with both themselves and their students. Good teaching is a blend of attitude, knowledge, motivation, and technique. Keeping a positive attitude in times of stress and exhibiting grace under pressure are important. Nor does demonstrating a sense of humor hurt. At tenure time, you may document your teaching skills in several ways. Most colleges rely on some form of standardized teaching evaluations as a primary indication of good teaching. Some encourage tenure candidates to submit course syllabi and to discuss any innovative teaching approaches used. Letters from former students can also be used to document teaching effectiveness. Such letters are particularly helpful if the students are practicing in a field relevant to the courses taught. For graduate teaching, letters from students who have gone on to achieve some career success themselves are useful.

Some colleges have instituted peer review of the classroom behavior of prospective tenure candidates. In such reviews, usually with forewarning, tenured faculty members attend one or more classes of the tenure candidate. The visiting faculty provide both verbal and written feedback, with the latter potentially becoming part of the tenure file. In addition to these written forms of evaluation, informal reputation and image management are important factors.

Having a Role Model: The Teaching Mentor

Having spent several years in higher education as a student, you likely can remember teachers you may wish to emulate as well as teachers who turned you off. Everyone who enters the teaching profession no doubt does this consciously or unconsciously. Terrific teachers share some characteristics. They care about students. They care about their subject matter and know it well. And they care about motivating students to learn.

Teachers who are duds also share certain characteristics. They lack empathy for or understanding of the student condition. They blame students for not learning rather than share blame for not motivating students. They make simple material complex. Duds make interesting subject matter uninteresting. They are unapproachable, cold, and icy. They speak in a monotone. In short, they are the worst that a teacher can be: boring.

Ideally, professors would be taught to teach in graduate school, just as elementary and secondary teachers are taught to teach in undergraduate school. Thus prospective professors would be encouraged to think about the elements of good teaching before they even reach the classroom rather than addressing teaching as a postdoctoral afterthought and even nuisance as is sometimes the case now. In the best of all possible worlds, fledgling professors would have had a teaching mentor in graduate school—someone under whom they apprenticed and from whom they learned about class dynamics.

In this ideal scenario, the director of the doctoral program or the departmental graduate committee would have assigned you to a professor in your field or subfield. The professor would act as a mentor by helping you become a better teacher in addition to possibly providing research guidance. In some doctoral programs, teaching assistants now sit in on a professor's class throughout the semester taking notes, grading papers, and generally watching and learning how to be effective and how to handle problems that arise in class. The primary purpose of this, however, is to assist the professor in teaching his or her own class, rather than to teach the graduate student how to teach future classes.

A more active mentoring role by professors currently assigned teaching assistants could enhance awareness of good teaching skills in the next cohort of young professors. Teaching mentors would invite their graduate students to drop by and ask questions about how to handle various classroom situations. They would share with their graduate students special techniques for stimulating debate and discussion. Mentors would also explain to assigned graduate students their grading philosophies and how evaluation of students is often linked to student evaluation of teachers.

Unfortunately, you likely had neither a preparatory class in teaching nor a teaching mentor in graduate school. Like many junior faculty, you may learn teaching techniques through trial and error, often making embarrassing and painful mistakes in the process. As a prospective tenure candidate, however, you can ill afford a reputation for bad teaching. Once you have been labeled as mediocre or even worse, such an image is hard to change. A negative teaching image can injure your chances for tenure and your professional reputation, placing you at a disadvantage with other colleagues, some of whom may be fiercely competitive.

Short of sexual harassment or racial slurs in class, any single mistake in teaching is not likely to be fatal to your prospects of getting tenure. But a string of mistakes undercuts your case for tenure. If mediocre or negative reviews or student complaints indicate that you have a teaching problem, then you should work to change your method or approach and try to improve communication with students.

Developing a Record to Meet the Teaching Criterion

Developing teaching skills and a record that is supportive of tenure is important. In major research universities, failure to be an adequate teacher may, along with other weaknesses, result in dismissal. Being an outstanding teacher will not get you tenure if you have a deficient publishing record, but if you have a borderline publication record that is viewed as weak in quantity of publications, then being an excellent or outstanding teacher may tip the balance in your favor. In close calls, teaching can make a difference. By contrast, in smaller colleges, teaching may be the dominant criterion for tenure. In either setting you can ill afford to ignore it. Here are some tips to think about as you develop a teaching record for tenure. (See Table 6.1.)

Table 6.1 Developing a Tenurable Teaching Record

To develop teaching skills and a record as a good teacher:
  Do not take criticisms personally.
  Teach to your strengths.
  Treat students with respect.
  Allocate time to students outside the classroom.
  Develop motivational skills and substantive knowledge.
  Pay attention to grading and student feedback.
  Take student evaluations of your teaching seriously.
  Troubleshoot teaching problems as quickly as possible.
  Present yourself as a concerned and dedicated teacher.
  Save all student evaluations and peer reviews of your teaching and
    any supportive letters from students.

Not Taking Criticism Personally

To improve on teaching and to obtain good teaching evaluations, some dispassionate introspection is helpful as well as an ability to hear criticism and not take it personally. It is never easy to get back student evaluations and read comments that are harshly critical or unfair. An essential part of teaching maturity is the capacity to weigh and evaluate what students have said and to use it to improve in the future.

Poor student evaluations are not always indicative of poor teaching. Some students may misrepresent what occurs in the classroom. Some may only award good teaching scores to those teachers who are "easy" and give them high grades. And some courses, particularly required courses that are heavily quantitative, may be harder to teach because students have a fear of and resistance to the subject matter. Of course, these factors should be considered in determining a response to student evaluations.

Teach to Your Strengths

In departments with flexibility in establishing teaching schedules, you may find it expeditious to shift whenever possible to teach courses in your areas of strength. Some strengths involve teaching styles and formats. Some faculty members excel at teaching large lectures, a format that requires the professor to be part entertainer, part teacher, and part scholar. The professor is literally "on stage." An ability to be humorous, find poignant analogies, and present material in a highly organized fashion are important in this format.

Often discussion is limited or not possible, and the professor must be able to capture the attention of the lecture attendees for a minimum of 50 minutes. Large lectures require attention to voice intonation, speaking style, and delivery, as well as to subject matter. Large lectures also require effective management of teaching assistants in some settings.

Other faculty members excel at small, intensive seminars, where stimulating discussion and personal interaction with the students are important. Teaching skill in this setting can be more Socratic than the didactic format of large lectures. Effective teachers "bring out" the students and encourage them to learn to articulate ideas coherently and effectively. Much interpersonal skill is helpful, including an ability to listen to what students are saying and responding in a manner that enhances learning.

Although some faculty members are effective at undergraduate teaching, others excel more at graduate teaching. The former learn to boil down material to present it simply. The latter are immersed in the current literature of the field and are likely to be active researchers. In some departments both graduate and undergraduate programs exist and provide junior faculty with options to "teach to their strengths."

Another type of strength is substantive expertise. Here you are well advised before tenure to develop a reasonable number of courses that you teach well and stick to them. Even if you are curious about other subfields and wish to expand into new areas, resist doing so until after you have tenure. Before tenure, your time is better spent teaching and refining courses you do well and developing your tenure record in other areas, especially publishing. Of course, in smaller departments you will necessarily be called on to teach a broader array of courses. You must be willing to do so, within reason, or you will be perceived as not a good department citizen. You do not, however, want to become the person to whom the department chair turns every time there is a course no one else is willing to teach. Nor do you wish to teach every course in the college catalog in your department, at least not before tenure. Teaching to your substantive strengths allows you to establish your best record in teaching and to have time for other aspects of your tenure record.

Treating Students With Respect

You should beware of *arrogance*, a disease of the profession, particularly among newly minted Ph.D.s. The disease erodes teaching effectiveness and hurts prospects for tenure in most settings. Junior faculty members who have this disease can be recognized in several ways. Often they are heard grumbling that the students do not match the quality of those that they had during their ABD days of teaching. Lack of student comprehension rising in part from poorly structured and thought-out lectures is blamed on the low mental capacity of students, who are "not bright enough." Universities and colleges do vary in the training and skills of incoming students, so on occasions the complaints of junior faculty about the inadequate training and performance levels of students have some merit. Some schools will have an average triple-digit SAT score among their student body, and other schools will average quadruple SAT scores. But there are many other reasons why students do not meet performance expectations of junior faculty. Most large undergraduate classes will include some proportion of freshmen. Young freshmen or even experienced adults who are reentering school after a long layoff are less adept at studying or sorting out important information from trivia, so more patience and time must be devoted to them. Good student-teacher relationships take time to cultivate.

It is futile to gripe that students at state colleges do not match those at Harvard, Yale, or even a flagship state university, a common complaint of arrogant new teachers. Junior faculty members have little control over institutionwide admissions criteria. As a larger share of students attend college, those with lower test scores will necessarily be admitted. The emphasis in recent years on diversity may also lead to greater disparities in junior faculty expectations and skills exhibited by students, reflecting past inequities and educational declines at the secondary level.

Good teacher-managers accept the level of student they have at their respective institutions, whether that be an elite college or a community college. The goal of the good teacher-manager is to raise the level of student performance to as high a level as possible, given their initial skills and abilities. Good teachers encourage students to achieve levels they otherwise would not.

If you constantly grumble about the quality of students at your institution, at tenure time senior colleagues may conclude that you do not know how to relate to "our kind of student." Even a superior publishing record may not overcome negative feelings other faculty members hold toward you for constantly putting down the students. In the short run, junior faculty members who are upset with undergraduate student capacities have options that are preferable to complaining before senior faculty members. One is to announce early in the class during the drop-add period the amount of work required and the extensiveness of writing assignments and other projects. This strategy encourages students who have little interest to drop the course and seek an easier one.

New Ph.D.s often are accustomed to the rigor of graduate courses from which they have just come, and sometimes they have difficulty lowering their expectations to an undergraduate level. Thus a second approach is to adjust so to cover less material more thoroughly.

A third approach is to give redundant work until students perform the assignments correctly. This is time-consuming, but it engenders much less ill will than giving bad grades to an entire class, which is almost always a bad strategy. Most serious students will appreciate the chance to redo work that was not done as expected the first time. This allows you to generate an image of yourself as a conscientious, demanding, but fair teacher who is concerned about students. If you are still frustrated with student performance, then you might pursue a more drastic strategy: seek employment at other colleges with higher admissions standards.

Allocating Time to Students Outside the Classroom

To demonstrate that you care about student intellectual development, try to have an open-door policy at least part of the time. This means explaining office hours to the students and inviting them to visit in those periods to talk about the class or any problems they may be having in it. When they see you in your office and actually talk with you outside of class, they see you in more in human terms. If you are accessible, concerned, and show students you care about them, they may even grow to like you. There is nothing unethical about being liked. Yet enthusiastic and youthful professors should guard against encouraging crushes and infatuations that some students may develop. Do this by focusing on intellectual topics and avoid discussing your own personal affairs.

Meeting with students during regular, predictable office hours establishes a comfort zone. Let students know that you are accessible and approachable and are willing to develop a relationship that will allow you to enhance their intellectual growth and development. But you are their mentor and teacher, not their buddy or date. If they temporarily forget the difference, you should not.

Interactions with graduate students may be more intense as you guide major seminar papers, serve on thesis and dissertation committees, and advise them on career options. Yet the basic principles of an open-door policy that applied to undergraduate students also applies to graduate students.

Developing Motivational Skills
and Substantive Knowledge

Like a manager of a football or basketball team, teachers are in the business of motivation. Any good manager knows that for his team or employees to do well, they have to be psyched up. Many students, especially the younger, undecided students, lack motivation. Some do not know why they should be studying fruit flies in a jar, esoteric statistics, or great thinkers of various traditions when there are more interesting things to study—like the opposite sex. Some do not know why they should deny their desires to go to the fraternity party just because their teacher promises them an exam they will never forget. Many new undergraduates have not learned to set priorities or how to manage all their free time. Some students do not know how to channel their energies in a productive way. They are lost in the wilderness of campus life, where free choices are abundant.

Good teachers strive to find ways to motivate their students. Most good teachers use a combination of carrots and sticks. Students receive rewards for academic achievement and fear the consequences of not performing up to expectations. To be effective motivators, goals set for students by the teacher in the form of assignments, workloads, and tests must be challenging yet realistic. Feedback must be timely and fair.

The challenges of becoming a good teacher are complicated by the fact that many students are in transition from one stage of life to another, often questioning themselves and their abilities. Some students have a built-in inferiority complex. They lack self-confidence. The least fortunate and most insecure have begun to believe what other teachers have bred in them for years—that they are limited and ignorant and will forever be that way. It is not easy to motivate anyone, but motivating such students may be particularly difficult.

Motivation is a skill that is highly desired in almost every sector of life. There are many motivational styles, so it is almost easier to identify behaviors that do not motivate than those that do. Students are not motivated by teachers who talk down to them or who treat them with disrespect. Many students dislike the so-called easy teacher, especially at advanced undergraduate and graduate levels. The students may feel that such teachers are condescending and boring.

Good teacher-managers begin using their motivation techniques at the first class meeting and set the tone for the rest of the course. They usually start out by explaining to their students how the students can make this course work for them. For example, it is useful to discuss the art of listening with students—that students must be willing to learn and to listen to others. Students have unique experiences and can make contributions to the class by sharing their insights about the readings. Peer learning is important in the classroom, and the good teacher-manager makes this point immediately. They explain to their class that one student may enhance another's understanding of the material and reinforce an understanding at the same time by asking questions or making comments.

Establish a symbiotic relationship with students on the first day of class. It is useful to say, "It is my responsibility to raise challenging and interesting questions, to present material in a stimulating manner. But you, too, have a responsibility, not only to be present in body, but also to be responsive and listen carefully to the thoughts of others. You, too, are a participant and have duties to make this class work for you."

At times, despite your best efforts you may find student motivation difficult. For one reason or another, perhaps poor classroom chemistry, you may feel alienated from a particular class or may begin to dread going to it. As a result, you may shut off discussion and send out signals that frighten normally talkative students into passivity. They, in effect, act out their hostility and alienation in class. Remember that it is not always your fault when classes are not responsive.

Paying Attention to Grading and Student Feedback

A major factor affecting student-teacher relations is the grading of exams or other classroom projects. It is important when you first begin teaching to check with department colleagues about the amount of work they assign. Although you do not want to have their approach to teaching dictate yours, you do not want the amount of work you assign to be too far from the norms used by your colleagues. If you assign excessive work compared to the norms, students may try to avoid your classes and complain vigorously to your colleagues if they cannot. If you assign too little work relative to the norms, some senior faculty members may see you as lazy or as trying to curry favor with students with light workloads to get good student reviews.

The format of your class may dictate or at least partially determine the type of exam you use. Large lecture sections mean that much or all of the exam must be standardized. Smaller classes allow essay exams, papers, and more intensive projects. Students expect and even demand grades and other feedback on their work within a reasonable period of time. Few things will sour relations with a class more quickly than not paying attention to student grades and feedback. Bend over backwards to make your grading reasonable and fair.

New undergraduate students may not know how to prepare for an upcoming exam. Teaching students according to the material that will be on the exam is usually boring and possibly unethical. On the other hand, helping students prepare for the exam is not. Such help may include putting a sample copy of an old exam on reserve in the library, setting up time outside of class for review sessions in a question-and-answer format, using available computer programs that allow students to get a hands-on perspective on a study question, and inviting students to your office to ask substantive questions about the reading material. Such effort could be time-consuming, but good student evaluations are a likely outcome.

Professors who have exhausted every motivational tool at their disposal may still confront students who perform poorly. In such settings, when all other avenues have been exhausted, the faculty member has little option but to fail the student who cannot do adequate work. Carrots should take precedence over sticks, but not to the point of gaining a reputation as a patsy. All carrots and no sticks will result in ineffective teaching.

Feedback on student work and projects is essential to good motivation. Take the time to make clear, concise, and constructive comments on exams and papers. Be prompt when returning exams and assignments and do not be sloppy. Students need to know how they are doing. Few things are more frustrating to a student than to get back an exam or paper with unreadable, undecipherable remarks. They may perceive that the professor cared little about their performance and decide that the remarks are not worth pursuing in the first place.

Sound and clear grading policies are important to student-teacher relations. If grading objectives are not clear and grading is perceived as arbitrary, a poisonous classroom atmosphere may develop in which some students may begin to feel that the professor is inaccessible and unfair. Highly motivated and ambitious students are particularly concerned about grades. Objectives that students should meet before attaining a certain grade and the criteria for grading must be clearly articulated. These objectives and criteria are preferably laid out in syllabi and are clear from the beginning of the class.

Good teachers find a way to make student projects appealing to them as well as to their students. When making assignments, incorporate research or intellectual interests. Good teacher-managers, like other good managers in the public and private sector, find a way to develop commonalities with their working partners. Instead of emphasizing differences, stress similarities: Students will identify more with you if you do this. Assign paper topics that overlap with research that you have already done; this way you will be more interested as well as more knowledgeable about what students write. When appropriate and when there is overlap, discuss your research with your student. Again, this will engender more enthusiasm from you, and your students will sense your genuine interest. Good teacher-managers want to establish a certain atmosphere in the classroom, one that projects openness, preparedness, enthusiasm, and common interests.

Student Evaluations of Your Teaching: Taking Them Seriously

By all means, take student evaluations seriously, because others who pass judgment on your tenure will. Student evaluations may reflect more accurately how you are communicating with your students than how well and how much you are teaching them. Critics of teaching evaluations argue that they measure popular rather than good teaching. But despite their drawbacks, most universities and colleges use evaluations as a major indication of teaching quality both in annual reviews and at tenure. Teaching evaluations are typically included in your tenure file.

Students often reward popular teachers with good evaluations and overlook or give lower evaluations to the less jovial, but still good teacher. The categories of popular teacher on the one hand and good teacher on the other hand do overlap, but this is not always the case. Popular teachers, however, do tend to get good evaluations. They hold court in the classroom. They tell scintillating jokes and heart-stopping war stories. They take a personal interest in their students and revel in student attention and student-related activities.

Popular teachers have class overload; every student wants their classes even if they are unrelated to his or her major. They keep steady and long office hours, and they usually have a line of students waiting to see them during every week. They are disgustingly happy, happy, happy. They often identify more with the students than they do with their sometimes less friendly and less jovial colleagues, who are strapped to the computers or prefer no more human contact than is absolutely necessary.

Good teaching and popular teaching share some similarities. Demonstrating an interest in your students is the most important. Empathy and accessibility are also very important. The good teacher, who is an expert in his or her field, is also long on substance. Making that substance attainable and understandable in a creative and imaginative way is the key to combining popular teaching and good teaching. A good teacher, unlike a popular teacher, may not dwell on entertainment per se, but a good teacher will try to convey useful information and knowledge to students in a lucid and innovative way. A good teacher will not do all the thinking for the student. Instead, good teachers when possible use the Socratic method, stimulate group discussion, use computer simulations, and formulate debate teams. These deviations from the straight lecture format give the students a chance to think independently and give the teacher a chance to demonstrate versatility and innovation in the classroom. Certainly some popular teachers may be short on substance, but they are long on style and grace in the classroom. They are the teachers that many academics love to hate; they provoke jealousy from less charismatic teachers. Being a popular teacher is not crucial to getting tenure, but it does not hurt. You certainly do not want to strive to be unpopular. A judicious balance of good teaching and student acceptance of your teaching style is better than total emphasis on popularity. Documenting that you have this balance will be helpful in meeting the teaching criterion for tenure.

Troubleshooting Teaching Problems

To avoid problems in your teaching record, you must be prepared to diffuse potentially troublesome situations in the classroom as quickly as possible. In almost every class, there is an ornery student—the dreaded troublemaker. Nobody likes to anticipate trouble, but doing so may enhance survival. A troublesome student can alter the image that other students have of you. They may perceive you as a wimp or as an unbearable tyrant simply by the way you handle troublesome, aggravating circumstances. A troublesome student can make the atmosphere in the course unbearable, unless he or she is handled properly.

One kind of troublemaker is the student who craves total attention. Such students behave in a way that implicitly or even explicitly demands that the class and the teacher give them an undue and unwarranted amount of attention. This type is often goofy and funny. Attention-grabbing students may try to dominate class discussions, crack jokes loudly, make suspicious noises in the back of class, and otherwise devise spectacles to get attention. This troublemaker is usually harmless but may daunt new teachers. One way to diffuse attention grabbers is to give them the attention they want, within limits. Inside the classroom, let him or her speak, but switch to other students when he or she begins to ramble. Outside of class, ask the troublemaker to meet with you to try to get at the root of the problem. Explain that there are other students in the class who need time, attention, and a chance to perform as well. When possible, ignore inappropriate attention-grabbing maneuvers or treat them humorously in class rather than give them more weight by taking them seriously. With time and patience, behaviors of this kind can be modified. If, however, the antics of the attention grabber are not modified and are disruptive to the learning of other students, then you may have to ask the attention seeker to leave.

Another kind of troublemaker is the type who is outwardly hostile or sarcastic. This type of troublemaker unreasonably challenges everything you say. You may hear snide comments about your lecture whispered loudly in the back of the class. He or she will actively try to nurture classroom insecurities or resentments about tests and other assignments and will seek to foster insurrection in the classroom. This student wants to hurt you, even if you have done nothing to him. Fortunately, this type of troublemaker is quite rare.

This student may be mentally unbalanced and even frightening. A sense of humor may not work with this troublemaker. The insurrectionist, who is deadly serious about making life harder for you and the serious students in your class, has no scruples and generally has no real desire to learn. Catch the insurrectionist early; make an example of him or her to the rest of the class. Demonstrate clearly that these tactics will not be tolerated. Ask this student to leave and to return only when his or her problems are ironed out. In other words, save yourself some grief.

Occasionally, inexperienced teachers (or even experienced ones) start off on the wrong foot with a class. You may have a raging headache on the first day of class because of an argument with your spouse at breakfast and be irritable and snap at a student who asks a question. You may sound like Attila the Hun on the first day, aggressively telling students how many other students you have flunked in the past and how you still feel like flunking many more. You may miss the first week of classes because of a professional conference and students may be confused as a result.

When you make a mistake or when something happens that dispels classroom harmony, acknowledge it. Tell the class that you misstated a fact (if that was the case) and correct yourself immediately. If you came across wrong on a particular day and you realize it or a student brings it to your attention, then make amends with your class with an apology or restate what you said in a less offensive way. Above all, do not let your personal problems spill over into the class; do not take out your problems on your students. Like an actor who does not let personal problems affect stage performances, a good teacher enters the classroom with enthusiasm each day and puts personal problems aside for the moment.

Presenting Yourself as a Concerned and Dedicated Teacher

How you show yourself to the world, including your department colleagues, affects their image of you and your eventual success. Tenure candidates can shape how others see them by either stressing their own strengths and playing down their weaknesses—the professorial version of "putting your best foot forward." While you are ill advised to hide or lie about weaknesses, you are equally ill advised to advertise faults and play up weaknesses.

Being a good teacher is one area relevant to meeting the criteria for tenure. Perceptions are often as important as reality. It is important to control and manage your teaching image. The criteria and methods that are used to measure good teaching will always be subjective. Whether your department relies solely on student evaluations or whether it combines student evaluations with peer evaluations from other faculty, someone will be interpreting and judging in very subjective ways what good teaching is. Therefore, it is up to the individual teacher to project and maintain an image that is appealing to colleagues and students.

First, become familiar with the survey instrument that is designed to measure your teaching effectiveness. You may not actually teach to the instrument by rearranging your presentations to evoke certain responses from the students when they take the survey, but you do want to know how you are being judged. Most surveys ask about qualities that are important to teaching such as your preparedness, your clarity in explaining concepts, your knowledge of the subject being taught, and the level of organization in your lectures. Other common questions are whether critical thought was encouraged, whether the instructor was open to new viewpoints, whether discussion was stimulated, and whether assignments and exams were graded fairly and returned promptly. Did you explain course objectives at the beginning of the course? Were you available outside of class? The question that often receives the most attention in evaluations of teaching asks if, overall, the instructor was effective. (See Table 6.2.)

Some survey instruments are open-ended and simply ask students to identify the course's best features, worst features, and needed improvements. There are techniques that some

Table 6.2 Common Questions on Standardized Teaching Evaluations

The standard teaching evaluation may ask about your competency in these areas:

preparedness
clarity in explaining concepts
knowledge of the subject being taught
level of organization in lectures
encouragement of critical thought
openness to new viewpoints
stimulation of discussion
prompt return of assignments and exams
explanation of course objectives at beginning of course
availability outside of class
effectiveness and value as teacher

teachers use to improve their performance on these instruments; they range from telling jokes before the instrument is administered (allowable) to intercepting bad evaluations and throwing them in the waste basket (unacceptable).

After you have become familiar with what is expected of your teaching, you then want to build a record and an image of good teaching. When building a record of good teaching, it is wise to keep a list of innovative techniques that you have used in class that succeeded in spurring valuable class discussion and student questions. You should maintain a file of these techniques, which may vary from classroom simulations to computer programs, from unusual class formats to group discussions and debates. Keep a folder of these for purposes of documenting your teaching skills when you are considered for tenure. Keep letters of praise from students; keep records of your advising responsibilities and the number of students you advised. In general, give the appearance of interest in teaching even if you prefer the company of computers to students.

To promote and maintain the image of a good teacher, emphasize your good qualities in discussions with colleagues and more advanced students. These qualities might include fairness (treating every student alike when grading exams, regardless of the student's personality or difference of opinion with you). Other qualities you might stress are your caring and desire to see your students succeed and your willingness to engage in discussion and to explain material clearly.

Saving Your Teaching Evaluations

Save *all* of your student evaluations and peer evaluations. If early reviews were not that positive, use them to show how much you have improved. If you do not save less favorable evaluations, then it will look as if you doctored your record, and your colleagues will question the accuracy of your image. If most of your evaluations are reasonable, your colleagues will understand the limits of evaluation instruments and know that some teaching qualities cannot be measured.

Although teaching evaluations by students and peers are not perfect, you should take them as seriously as you would like students to take their grades. Your image as a teacher and your success at attaining tenure may depend on it.

7 | Meeting the Service Criterion

Everyone in academics knows that tenure and promotion are based on performance in three areas: teaching, research, and service. Nevertheless, service has typically been the criterion that people think about the least, often waiting until the very last minute. As the preparation of the tenure file proceeds, one common question a faculty member may ask is "What have I done that I can call service?" Another common idea is that no one was ever not tenured or promoted for lack of service, a small comfort to those who have not given service much thought until the time to prepare the tenure and promotion file.

A faculty member who plans further ahead may begin to think about what he or she has done that could be called service in the spring of the year before the tenure file is due. He or she may then talk to a friend, a senior faculty member in the same or a different department or the department chair and ask, "What counts as service, anyway?" or "Maybe you should appoint me [or suggest my name] for several committees this coming year, so I have them on my record."

Certainly, if you are reading this book, you are not planning to think about most aspects of tenure and promotion at the last minute. Most assistant professors should think about service at the beginning of their appointment as an assistant professor. Just as with teaching and research (and maybe more so), there are tips and hints that may be explored in advance to provide a candidate with a tenurable range of service experiences.

Moreover, not all service needs to be thought of as drudgery that gets you nowhere. Through service activities, faculty members can learn useful things about the local or university community, network with other faculty members in the university and other people in their field, and play an important role in general public education. In addition, activities that count as service for the university may include the types of participation in voluntary associations that many people perform for their own intrinsic reward and as part of being good citizens and neighbors.

This chapter will first review the different ways in which service can be viewed and then review different types of service activities and how they can help build a career in various ways as well as meet the service criterion. The chapter will also identify traps to avoid about service, particularly at the beginning stages of an academic career.

How Various Universities and Colleges View Service

All universities and colleges include service as one criterion for promotion and tenure, but its importance varies with the institution. In many universities, the standards for meeting the service criterion are quite low, requiring little more than being agreeable and serving on a few mandatory committees within the department—normal expectations placed on an assistant professor. In other universities and colleges, service expectations exist for all ranks of faculty. These expectations may include specified categories, such as department, school, university or college, community, and professional. As in other areas of activity, prospective tenure candidates are well advised to determine what the service requirements and norms are in their specific department and university.

Determining departmental norms will be relatively easy in some situations, because some universities require written standards for tenure and promotion. In those cases, the different types of service activities expected are usually specified. Brief conversations with colleagues will give the new faculty member some sense of the amount of service expected within each area. Solicited advice on specific categories is usually ignored at the potential peril of the tenure candidate.

If a university does identify different specific types of service (department, campuswide, community, or professional) on its written tenure-evaluation form, wise tenure candidates develop a service activity within each category. Particularly for universities that have specific tenure and promotion forms that list each type of service with a space to fill in activities, the same rules are relevant as those that apply to student tests. If at all possible, leave no blanks. This requires advance familiarity with any such forms and a strategy for performing some minimal type of service activity in each category.

Tenure candidates in universities and colleges in which there are no clear written standards about service (and possibly about other aspects of tenure and promotion) confront greater ambiguity and potential difficulty. A new faculty member should try to develop some knowledge of what service standards are, preferably soliciting information from a variety of sources—the department chair, senior colleagues, and other junior faculty members. Having many sources of information will help determine whether consensus prevails about the role of service or whether fellow faculty members' opinions vary, depending on how much service they themselves perform. Sensitivity to this variation alerts tenure candidates to different evaluation strategies other faculty members in the unit may use to evaluate whether the tenure candidate has met the service criterion.

The service criterion is different in degree from the teaching and research criteria: Its evaluation may be the most subjective. In evaluating the scholarship criterion, publishing results in articles and books that can be counted, even if faculty disagree on the relative prestige of a publication outlet. In assessing the teaching criterion, most campuses today require some uniform type of evaluation form to be completed by students at the end of each class. Thus, for teaching at least some piece of likely standardized quantitative information will be available.

Evaluating the service criterion is far more subjective. Obviously, evaluators can do some counting of the amount of service activity. In fact, prospective tenure candidates should keep clear records of each service activity in which they engage. But counting the number of activities alone is insufficient proof that the standard for service has been met. Critical evaluators may contend that the tenure candidate's service activities involved little time or effort. Critics may also argue that the tenure candidate was not cooperative or pleasant about performing the service activities and had to be coerced into doing service. Others may argue that the candidate should have done more and had a more varied amount of service activity. Thus service is one tenure criterion for which tenure candidates need to carefully manage their image.

Service is one way of showing that a faculty member is a good citizen or a team player. Attitude counts, although departments differ on the importance of attitude. Few department chairs, however, will consider tenure candidates outstanding in service if they are always negative about every committee assignment and stress how much they do not want to perform the suggested service task. Department chairs often have responsibility for the distribution of activities to committees, and they want their faculty members to help share the burden and to participate in the decision making.

In many departments, the chair may view service as more important than do other faculty members. Do not ignore the chair's opinion on this. Because chairs often write a separate letter and have a separate vote, some special consideration about the chair's opinion of service is useful (refer to Chapter 3 for the discussion of the tenure file and the tenure process).

Also, university- or college-level review committees often place more weight on the chair's statement about service than on those of other faculty, figuring that the chair is in the best position to judge the willingness with which campus service is performed and the quality of effort and quantity of time expended.

Some departments exude a sense of boredom with and disdain for service activities. Faculty members chat among themselves about how they got out of service on a certain committee or just never attended meetings. For the young assistant professor, it may be dangerous to engage in such conversations. Although senior faculty members may find it amusing for their contemporaries to disparage service, such statements may be used in a negative manner at the time of a promotion decision for a junior colleague. In these discussions, the best rule for an assistant professor is to listen more and talk less.

Just as being negative on service in front of one's colleagues is a poor strategy for a new professor, so is being overly enthusiastic about it, especially in a department that emphasizes other activities such as research. Tenure candidates should remember to manage their service appearance. Being too eager could result in too many assignments and later be the basis for negative comments about productivity in other areas such as research. Examples of comments often heard include "She just spent too much time on committee work and it shows in her CV [curriculum vita]." Or, "He was very busy, but on the wrong things. All he ever talked about was his committee work; no wonder the number of publications is just too low."

All of these points return to the same major advice, which also is useful as one considers teaching and research. But because service is the least clear of the criteria in many places, the advice is particularly important in this area: Know your department. Understand the norms of your unit, your department chair, your dean, and others who will review the file. Understand its informal culture. Then figure out ways to meet those norms and to make service interesting and useful,

Table 7.1 Major Categories of Service

University Service
department
college
university
Community Service
public presentations
service on local boards or associations
general media appearances
alumni activities
Professional Service
activity in national or regional professional associations
manuscript and grant reviewing

not simply a burden to bear. Table 7.1 summarizes some of the general points about service for a beginning assistant professor.

Different Types of Service

Service includes a range of types of activities and levels. At the simplest level is service to the department and service on department committees. Moving outward into the broader university community, service activities can occur at the level of the school or college (whatever the unit beyond the department is called), or on overall university committees. Beyond this is service within the community. The definition of community can vary from place to place, but generally it will include at least the local area, town, or city; it often includes the whole state (especially at state-funded universities) and may include the nation for more prominent senior members of a department.

An additional type of service, which can occur at local, regional, or national levels, is service within the discipline and profession such as activities with various regional and national professional associations. This type of service can help to build a young scholar's reputation within the field and enhance a growing reputation based on research and scholarship. Again, Table 7.1 summarizes the major categories of each type of service, and these are discussed in greater detail in the following paragraphs.

Department Service

Not all departments are the same and not all provide the same range of service possibilities. In many small departments of fewer than eight faculty members, most decisions are handled by the total faculty or a committee of the whole. Thus few formal committees exist. In small departments, activities that would be handled through committees in a large department of 20 or more are performed by all faculty members. These activities include undergraduate curriculum, equipment and computer needs, search committees for new faculty positions, and selecting students to receive departmental honors. For tenure candidates in small departments, contributions to departmental activities in these areas may not easily show up as separate service, making it important to demonstrate some service beyond the departmental level. It is also important to find some way to include a description of these types of service activities so that universitywide committees, provosts, and even deans in large units are aware of the activity. One such place may be in the personal statement. The need for service beyond the department level is especially important if there is an overall tenure-evaluation committee at the school or university level that includes faculty from large departments who are used to many committee activities.

In contrast, for faculty in a large department, the most important and most expected service for junior faculty members may be on department committees. This chapter has already discussed the importance that departmental service may have to the department chair. Similarly, senior faculty members may view serving on minor departmental committees as the essential "dues" that a junior faculty member must

pay to become a full department member and a "team player."
Again, figure out what the expectations are in your unit and
then meet them.

One important aspect of department service is that the
quality of your performance of these duties will be more
visible to your colleagues than your work in other service areas.
Thus especially for department service, the willingness and
seriousness with which you perform these duties is as important as how much you do. Departmental committees, especially
in a large department, are one of the chief points of contact
with your colleagues. Such service provides an opportunity
to impress those colleagues with your knowledge, charm,
and good work (or an opportunity for them to form a negative opinion that could work against you). Remember the
principle of managing your image so that it is positive. Opportunities may arise for department service work that is not
as onerous as it appears to others. Such opportunities might
involve writing the first draft of a new curriculum or being
willing to take the first crack at developing the syllabus for a
new required course that you might end up teaching anyhow.
If you occasionally volunteer for such activities, you may
improve your image with important senior faculty. This will
be particularly true if senior faculty members and the chair
are concerned about having to coerce a faculty member into
doing a task. Taking on a few such tasks, especially when they
can be performed relatively quickly, may earn a new faculty
member much goodwill from the department chair and other
senior members who are spared from the activity. Especially
if the work is likely to end up assigned to you anyhow, agreeing
to do it before it becomes a 45-minute discussion in a department meeting may be a wise political decision at tenure time.

Administrative Levels Beyond the Department

Standards and expectations for service beyond the department vary greatly. At many major research-focused universi-

ties, such service is not expected or encouraged for junior faculty members. Rather, this type of service is expected once a faculty member has earned tenure for promotion from associate professor to full professor.

If tenure candidates receive a clear message from their departments that participation in activities beyond the department is a mistake for junior faculty members, they should probably heed that advice. It may well be helpful, however, to verify this with a few contacts in other departments in the university to be sure that the norms in your department are shared across the campus (check especially with junior faculty members in other departments to find out what their chairs are advising). If the department's norms are not shared, then it may be good to find one or two committee assignments at the college or university level to be able to list, although they should not be time-consuming. But do not talk much about these activities within your department, because they are not as valued there.

Probably a more typical situation is the university in which some service beyond the department is desirable, but everyone recognizes the primacy of teaching and research. In these cases, it is often helpful to seek out a committee assignment from a dean or associate dean or the chair of the faculty senate, depending on the level of committee. Such administrators (or faculty senate chairs) are usually very responsive to an inquiry from an assistant professor that states, "I really want to learn more about the overall university [or college], but know I need to focus on my teaching and research at this stage of my career. Is there a committee assignment that would give me a taste of such activities but not be overly burdensome before I achieve tenure and promotion?" Generally, the associate dean will find such a committee and often will have a positive memory of the faculty member as someone who wants to contribute beyond the department but thinks ahead and plans the use of his or her own time well. Remembering that part of tenure and promotion success involves image management, this strategy can be one way to develop a reputation as helpful, concerned, and forward-thinking. Service beyond the department level provides an opportunity to get to make contacts and network across the campus, perhaps to make new friends, and perhaps to meet the dean or other university-level administrators. In general, as a junior faculty member, unless your college is so huge that few faculty members have contact with the dean, you might want to occasionally check in with the dean and let him or her become better acquainted with you and your work.

Finally, think about the type of committee and work involved. Most universities have curriculum committees, often separated for undergraduate and graduate programs. These committees involve detailed work and exploration of syllabi and brief course descriptions, and they become very involved in administrative details. If this is work you like, it may be a good committee to serve on even though it meets frequently. It may also be a good committee at a slightly more advanced stage of career in which to test out your interest in departmental administration. If you hate this type of detail, avoid these types of committees because the appearance of being bored and distracted at meetings is not the reputation you wish to cultivate.

Other committees draw on other types of expertise. Budget committees require an ability to look at and examine financial details. They also may be a useful test of interest in departmental administration. If you find curriculum development uninteresting, but find the prospect of knowing more about the internal operation of the university exciting, then this type of committee service might be fun and educational, even though it involves real time commitments. Junior faculty members should avoid committees that may become involved in campuswide controversies, such as faculty athletic committees that can become a focus of attention if there are problems in the university's athletics department.

Community Service

Expectations about appropriate amounts and types of community service probably vary more than any other service area. This relates partially to differences across institutions. More important, different academic disciplines view community service in very different ways. For simplicity, this chapter contrasts three types of institutions: smaller colleges, public universities, and major private universities. In addition, differences between disciplinary fields and more applied or professional fields are contrasted.

Both smaller colleges and public universities are more sensitive to their communities. Smaller colleges are generally sensitive to both the specific local community, because that is often one source from which contributions are generated, and to the alumni community. For both groups, typical service expectations might be the willingness to give presentations on topics of more general public interest related to one's scholarly field of expertise. In addition, there might be other service expectations relating to service on boards of local agencies, especially if there is some connection between the area of academic expertise and the types of boards.

Depending on the size of the college and the department, few of these obligations may fall on or be expected of a junior person. If they are, typically a few a year are sufficient, and often, once a talk is prepared, the actual amount of time these service activities consume can be quite limited. The time commitment consists mostly of traveling to the site to give the speech and its actual delivery.

Other types of more recent service activities are requests for appearances on radio talk shows or other media settings. Most college faculty members do not consider these as constituting important service, although public relations offices on campus are interested in them. Some professional societies have also started columns in their newsletters that explicitly recognize interviews with the media or media recognition, although these often focus on national recognition. The importance placed on this type of media service varies. It is helpful to supplement with other types of service activities. Especially important are alumni and club presentations when the request originates with a higher-level administrator. For example, if the dean asks a junior faculty member to speak to an alumni group or the neighbor of the dean calls to ask if the faculty member can make a presentation at a local club, these are speaking obligations that one should try to meet. The image of being helpful and concerned about the image of the college in the community or with the alumni is important. Also, publicity about your research in the local community may lead to new research contacts (especially if you need entry into settings to conduct your research) or even to small pots of local funding for research.

Public universities often define their community more broadly than the local city or town. Especially for the flagship branch of the state university or for one of the major state-funded universities, the entire state may be viewed as an appropriate locale for service. Moreover, many public universities include service to the public and increasing the level of general education as part of their mission statements. Faculty members are public employees, and the obligation to provide speeches or advice to the state is real. Despite these origins, not only state universities but also departments within such universities differ. Sensitivity to departmental norms (and following such norms) is important.

Depending on the tenure candidate's field, requests to give talks or serve on state committees may be frequent or quite uncommon. Most departments at major universities have some commitment to protecting junior faculty members from too much of this type of service, which probably is not the wisest use of time early in one's career. However, specific requests from a department chair to give a community talk are probably best honored if possible. Being cooperative on small aspects of service is always good advice.

Tenure candidates who believe they are getting requests from community groups too often should discuss the problem with their department chair, asking for help in shifting the burden. Polite firmness may be necessary to avoid depleting energy on an excess of service when the research and scholarship criterion still has not been met. If excessive requests are relayed through colleagues (such as a senior faculty member suggesting that the new member talk to certain groups this year because the senior colleague has done it so often and is tired of it), point out that you have already done three of these this semester or that you are concerned about being able to finish a certain article or book within a necessary timeframe. One hopes that such polite firmness will diminish future attempts by a colleague to "dump" service activities on the newest junior faculty member.

Research-oriented private universities vary more on the extent to which they are involved with the local geographic community. Some have major areas of involvement, while others do not. Formally, however, there are important differences. These institutions view their recruitment base as regional or national and, unlike public universities, do not usually have an explicit mandate to serve the public of that state. At such institutions, service to community groups (within disciplinary fields) may receive little value. Assistant professors are often encouraged to avoid such activities and probably should do so in the initial stages of a career.

One type of service that is viewed as very important to large private universities is speaking to alumni groups in other locations; at the campus during parents' weekend, graduation, or homecoming; and leading special alumni activities, such as study tours. These activities are usually not asked of junior faculty members. If they are, it is probably a compliment about the interesting nature of one's research and a beginning reputation as an unusually interesting lecturer. If asked, the prospective tenure candidate should try to accommodate the requests.

Service to the community has a different interpretation in applied fields versus more disciplinary fields. Most of the comments in this section up to this point relate to disciplinary fields. For applied fields, service is often more important. Even if community service is not a more important explicit aspect of promotion and tenure criteria, the demands from the community for service are greater. In addition, contact with the community may be important in the development of field placements for students or sites for course projects. As some more disciplinary fields have begun to offer more explicitly applied tracks, such as the development of applied sociology majors or tracks relating to museum careers in history, this type of service is more valued. Community contacts become important for teaching as well as for service in both evolving disciplinary fields and traditionally applied fields.

In applied fields such as social work, public health, criminal justice, and public administration, a cadre of practitioners live and work in the local community and across the state. These practitioners hold various types of meetings and frequently need help in planning or evaluating new programs at work or understanding new trends in the field. A natural place to turn is to a faculty, especially one at a state university. Although departments vary, most hold the expectation that all faculty members should be helpful, pleasant, and open to these requests. Moreover, these practitioners are often very important to academic programs. If there is a graduate program in the area, the employees of these agencies who only hold a bachelor's degree are a major recruitment source for students. In addition, most of these programs require some type of internship or field experience, and thus relationships with local practitioner agencies are very important to maintain a list of available field placements. (See Table 7.2.)

Helping practitioners in applied fields may produce the additional benefit, as well as the potential liability, of professional visibility. Whether a new faculty member has been helpful to the local health department or county manager will

Table 7.2 Specific Aspects of Service in Applied Fields

Presence of local associations:
    Combine practitioners and academics.
    Expect some involvement with these groups.
    Be pleasant and noncondescending in these interactions.
    Groups may be a major recruitment source for students.
    Groups may provide needed entry into applied research settings.
Greater blurring of lines between community service and disciplinary
    service (and even teaching) than in nonapplied fields.
    May be helpful to include letters in your tenure and promotion files
    from local practitioners.
    Contacts may blur lines between service and teaching with supervi-
    sion of students for field placements.
    Former students are likely to become practitioner colleagues, sources
    of future students, and of research settings.

very likely be mentioned to more senior colleagues, particu-larly if the practitioners are displeased with their contact with the junior faculty member. In this type of service, as is some-times true with teaching, doing a good job may not receive much notice, but doing a bad job surely will. Thus this type of service should be taken seriously and done well. If not, it may have serious consequences to your total tenure and promo-tion decision.

Because of the frequent contact in applied fields between academics and practitioners, attitude and how service re-quests are turned down are quite important. It is quite accept-able to turn down a committee assignment on a task force on a certain problem in your area of expertise if the time for the meeting is already set and it conflicts with, or is too close to, a scheduled class time. If this is the case, however, the right answer when asked to serve on the committee, is to say, "I probably could have made a contribution to that committee, and picked up some useful insights as well, but I cannot neglect my obligations to students at that time." Although this nice answer will not generate positive comments back to your academic department, it will avoid the possible negative comments from such responses as "I am too busy" or even "I am too busy at this time" without a more detailed explanation. Similarly, practitioner sensitivity in applied fields to real or perceived slights from academicians should be acknowledged and treated with all the care of an undetonated land mine. Practitioners become upset if they believe the academics act superior or as if the field of practice does not matter. On the other hand, many practitioners appreciate the different time demands of academics. It is all right to turn down a request to speak locally because you have a major presentation at a national meeting the week after and you know you will need extra time to refine the talk and finish with data. To say, however, "I have something more important to do," or "I have to give an important talk a week later" sets the wrong tone, the type likely to result in a negative call to a dean or department chair.

For junior faculty members in applied fields, the line between community service and service within the disciplinary area is often blurred, especially at the local level. Serving as an officer in the local social work or public health association provides some mix between the type of professional association service discussed in the next section and more traditional community service. Usually, applied fields have local associations to which both the practitioner and academic community belong. Being active in such a group may not have the spinoffs of visibility to national colleagues and the development of a network of research colleagues, but it can benefit the faculty member in developing local research and placement contacts, as well as in creating a good citizen image in the professional area. Also, in applied fields, it frequently is helpful to have a few letters from practitioners at the time one develops the tenure file. Service in the local association is one positive comment that practitioners can make in such letters, along with comments on how helpful the faculty member has been on applied projects or special agency committees.

Professional Service Within Your Discipline or Field

This type of service is most likely to have direct positive benefits to the development of a tenure candidate's scholarship. Most faculty members wish to attain visibility within their discipline or profession. Scholarship is clearly one desirable way to accomplish this. It is not the only way, however, and being willing to serve on committees and as an officer in regional and national scholarly associations also helps to generate visibility. Because being active in associations forces you to go to meetings regularly, it is a way to make contacts with scholars at other universities. Scholars at other universities are the people who can write the essential external reference letters needed for the tenure file. If scholars elsewhere already know you and have talked to you personally about your research, then the letters may be richer in detail than if they have only read three of your papers sent to them a month before the external letters are due. Thus professional association service is one way that service can benefit other aspects of career development.

Not all roles in professional associations require the same amount of work. Junior faculty members should try to avoid those jobs that require a great deal of time, because the emphasis in early stages of the career must remain more focused on teaching and scholarship. Depending on the nature of the association (how large and whether it has a national or regional office), two time-consuming positions are often those of treasurer and newsletter editor. Being the chair or president is also time-consuming, but such an office also offers greater professional visibility.

Given the tight university budgets recently, another advantage of service and activity in professional associations is financial. Many departments have sharply limited travel funds. If a junior faculty member has both a scholarly paper to deliver and a service obligation at a national or regional meeting, the department may be more likely to allocate some of its travel funds to that person. Thus this service may have some direct monetary payoff, in addition to adding lines to the service portion of the curriculum vita and expanding the networks of scholars with whom one is personally acquainted.

There is one additional type of professional service: manuscript and grant reviewing. These types of service activities can help your own professional growth and keep you abreast of new research in the field. In addition, over time, the information that you are an on-time and thorough reviewer for several journals will itself become known and add to your academic reputation. For scholars, this is one of the most important types of service, because most scholarly journals could not continue to publish without these unpaid services.

Traps to Avoid and Special Circumstances

The general feeling about service among many faculty members is that it should be avoided because it drains away energy, effort, and creativity. Such negative consequences can occur in some situations, but they do not have to be the outcome of most activities. A little service in the early stages of a career is useful and, indeed, necessary. Too much is harmful.

Two groups of faculty often get called on too much and have trouble refusing service. On many campuses now, all committees want to be culturally sensitive and represent groups prominent in the entire student body. Thus each committee needs a woman and a minority faculty member. Because of past discrimination, there are not enough tenure-track faculty in these special categories on many campuses. New female and minority junior faculty members may be beseeched to serve on too many different committees, often with the plea that "We need your unique point of view represented." Such junior members need to learn to judiciously decline.

Beleaguered women and minority faculty members are helped in their efforts to avoid excessive committee assignments without creating ill will or a poor image if they have the support (and protection) of their department chairs. A supportive chair will inform the university that Professor X (the female or minority faculty member) is too busy completing scholarly projects to serve on additional committees. If a new committee is created on which Professor X's service is essential, it must be as a replacement for a current committee assignment. Even without this support, however, the faculty member must start saying no. At the time of tenure and promotion, service on six universitywide committees, four school committees, and four community groups will not substitute on most campuses for an adequate number of publications.

Another trap to avoid is a confusion between service and consulting. Often the lines are not clear. This may be especially true in some fields in which consulting opportunities are greater, such as business, psychology, and engineering. Tenure candidates must find out how paid consultation is viewed. In some universities, it may not be listed as service at all. In others it can be listed, but the form requires a specification of whether it was paid. If it was paid, then informal norms differ as to whether it counts. Too much paid consultation and no real service may, on some campuses, create an image of a tenure candidate as too money grubbing and not scholarly enough, especially if the publishing record is weak.

Changing Interactions Between a University and Its Community

Community and state support for higher education appears to be diminishing in many places. In the last few years, many have appeared arguing that professors teach too little and spend their time on arcane research projects that benefit no one. Most universities are becoming more concerned about their broader public image; this is especially true at state universities, where public support of higher education is critical to the allocation of state revenues.

Public image is becoming more important, and the faculty are one of the major groups that can help improve the university's image. Being sensitive to the public and being a good representative of the university's interests may grow in importance over the next few years. While the importance of scholarship and teaching will probably not diminish, the importance placed on service, especially community service, is likely to increase. Thinking ahead about the personal consequences at tenure time of these changing and expanding expectations will help a junior faculty member succeed.

8 | Paths to Tenure

How many career paths are there to tenure? The answer is many. We have observed at least six different but commonly used routes. Some are more desirable than others, but all work.

Paths Leading to Tenure

These six most common routes are known as (a) the superstar path; (b) the on-time, steady producer path; (c) the bounce-around path; (d) the fail-and-try-again path; (e) the late-career practitioner path; and (f) the late-career childrearing path.

The Superstar Path

The most desirable route to tenure is to be an academic superstar who is widely recognized as a precocious and brilliant achiever. We have known a few superstars who have achieved tenure early and unequivocally, almost always on the basis of scholarship. One superstar had more than 50 publications in almost every subfield in the discipline at tenure time. Another superstar had been a White House Fellow, had published several articles and a book, and was offered tenure after two years as an enticement to stay at the university. These cases, as well as others like it produce a "Wow!"

reaction among colleagues, who agree that the performance of the young scholar is outstanding and that tenure is deserved.

What constitutes superstardom may vary across fields. In public health, it make take as many as 25 peer-reviewed articles, with some in very good journals. In political science, a mere 10 articles may qualify if three are in the prestigious *American Political Science Review*, the lead journal in the field. In economics, three articles in the prestigious *American Economic Review* along with other publications would designate the author as a superstar. In history, a major widely reviewed and well-received book, along with accompanying articles and a second book in the works under contract would definitely make the scholar a superstar. In the sciences, such as chemistry or physics, external funding in addition to the number of articles would contribute to an assessment of superstardom by colleagues. Peer-reviewed funding from the National Science Foundation, along with starter money from professional associations and industry funds are among the funding sources that superstars may tap early in their careers.

Let us consider the case of Naomi, a superstar. Naomi earned a Ph.D. in sociology, writing a dissertation based on a data tape her advisor had. Naomi analyzed a part of the tape, writing chapters on each independent variable. At her defense, Naomi was criticized on the grounds the dissertation did not present a coherent whole or major test of theory. But once she graduated, Naomi quickly turned each semiautonomous chapter into a discrete article for publication. She got six articles out of her dissertation. Naomi's first tenure-track job was in a sociology department. As a medical sociologist, she quickly established contacts with the medical school. Within two years, she was offered the chance to switch to a tenure-track position there, an opportunity she took. She worked on large research projects as part of a team, efforts that also resulted in many publications. Naomi went up for tenure in her fourth year, and had almost 30 publications. She was awarded tenure at the end of her fourth year.

The On-Time, Steady Producer Path

Like superstardom, what constitutes on-time steady production varies by type of institution and field. At many research universities, 14 to 18 articles that are peer-reviewed, with one or two in the best journals or many in good journals, would qualify as on-time steady production. Some fields may substitute books for articles. In history in many research universities, one book and six to eight good articles would be considered on-time steady production.

The on-time steady producers we have known meet the tenure hurdles within the timeframe designated by AAUP rules, but they do not come up early. They are okay or better in every category considered for tenure. While colleagues look at the superstar and say "Wow!" their observations of the on-time steady producer are "No problems here." On-time steady producers have reasonable evaluations in teaching, are regarded as good department citizens, and have gained some recognition in regional associations. Their publication record is good.

David was an on-time steady producer before tenure. David worked in a mathematics department at a medium-sized state university. He tried to send out two articles a year for review and was generally successful at meeting this goal. When he went up for tenure, he had seven articles in print and three accepted for publication. David had good teaching reviews and had been a good department citizen. He was viewed as acceptable in all areas.

The Bounce-Around Path

We have known some colleagues to take a third path inadvertently and involuntarily: the so-called bounce-around or rolling-stone path to tenure. People on this path have a difficult time even landing a tenure-track job, sometimes through no fault of their own. Bounce-around scholars have a series of one-year jobs that are not tenure-track before landing one

130 I GETTING TENURE

that is. Some fields produce more bounce-around scholars than do others. We have known several such colleagues in history, English, literature, and foreign languages who eventually made it through the tenure process. In these fields there are often far more job candidates than tenure-track positions at any given time, especially in a recessionary market. A bounce-around pattern may evolve in other fields, however, including social sciences and education.

New scholars who cannot find a tenure-track position initially may bounce-around from one temporary position to another. Some patch together adjunct positions teaching courses part-time for two or more colleges at once. Their temporary and adjunct experience enables them to develop new courses and often a considerable portfolio of courses that they can teach. Their broad teaching repertoire eventually may lead them to a tenure-track position in the right setting. At some point, they may publish their dissertation, either in entirety or piecemeal in articles. This, plus frequently being the "inside candidate" at schools where they hold temporary or part-time positions enables them to eventually land a tenure-track position.

Because bounce-around candidates may not have even had a formal university office before landing a tenure-track job and were not permanent members of the departments in which they taught, they frequently have little professional service when they land their first tenure-bearing job. They must quickly establish a service record and an adequate number of publications. Often bounce-around scholars have the option of disregarding their teaching years before attaining a tenurable job in terms of the tenure clock. Therefore, bounce-around candidates may often have taught for several years longer than AAUP rules specify, because the years before acquiring the formal position may not count. Once on a tenure-track line, industrious and capable scholars then become on-time, steady producers.

Charles inadvertently ended up on a bounce-around tenure path. During his dissertation year, he began to apply for jobs in his field, 20th-century U.S. history. He was told that most of the tenure-track jobs for which he applied had anywhere from 100 to 400 other job applicants. When he came up empty-handed, his advisor managed to get him part-time teaching at the university where he was completing his Ph.D. He also taught two courses for a former teacher's college 30 miles away. The next year, a one-year replacement opened up at the teacher's college. Charles worked there full-time. The following year he found a one-year replacement position at a small liberal arts college 100 miles away. During the year, a tenure-track position opened up at the liberal arts college. Charles applied, along with 100 others. Because the faculty knew Charles and liked him, he made the interview list. The faculty felt Charles could meet their needs and he was finally hired for the tenure-track position. Once he had this position, he began to build a tenurable record.

The Fail-and-Try-Again Path

This approach to tenure is sometimes expected in the Ivy League, where young professors go to gain prestige from having worked early in their careers at Harvard, Yale, Princeton, and so on. Because such universities tenure only a few professors in any decade, at least some junior professors are expected to leave after five years and before their tenure decision so that new assistant professors may be recruited. Some portion of those who do not leave voluntarily will be rejected at tenure. Junior scholars denied tenure then seek new positions as assistant professors in less prestigious universities but with the advantage of the experience and publications they gained during their time in the Ivy League.

Junior scholars at less prestigious universities may also inadvertently follow this tenure path if they are denied tenure in their first job. Because tenure is institution-specific, being denied tenure at one location does not mean that the scholar will never gain tenure. It does mean, however, that the person must try again at some other college or university, usually one of lesser prestige. Lucky candidates who are trying again are able to land another tenure-track position at a university of about the same quality. Howard was one scholar we knew who tried again. He started out his career at a major Western university. After five years of steady production, he was told he probably would be denied tenure. His scholarly publications had not been high enough, plus he had been on the losing end of an ongoing factional battle within the department.

Howard was a good teacher and had an adequate service record. He was able to secure another tenure-track position at a flagship school in a Southern state. He spent five more years there compiling a tenurable record and went up for tenure there in his sixth year. In his second school, when he tried for tenure a second time, Howard was able to gain the department's support. He was told that he had adequate total production, but there was some concern that when the production was averaged across the years he had been out teaching, the number of publications per year was not very high. Nonetheless, Howard squeaked through the university-level committee and was awarded tenure in his eleventh year of teaching. Howard was a particularly pleasant colleague and was noncontroversial in demeanor and behavior. Had he been controversial, his low annual publication rate could have been used as justification to turn him down.

The Late-Career Practitioner Path

This path to tenure is mostly used in applied fields, such as health, business, public administration, and sometimes law. While women in nursing and social work may also use this path on occasion, more commonly those who follow the late-career practitioner path to academic tenure are men. Sometimes men who are leaving military careers also take this path.

People on this path usually are doing well in their practitioner jobs but reach a midlife crisis or turning point and decide to pursue a new but related career. They return to school and earn a doctorate, sometimes while still working. Once in a tenure-track position, people on this path relate well to practitioners and usually rise in service functions and activities quickly. They often are sought out by practitioners and the community to provide access to research settings and expertise. Once in a tenure-track job, many people on this career path often become on-time, steady producers. More marginal tenure candidates in this tenure path find that their previous experience and contacts may enable them to make it through the process by better understanding institutional politics and using contacts they otherwise would not have had.

Jason illustrates this path to academic tenure. After receiving his undergraduate degree in business administration, he worked in a hospital's financial office. He wished to advance but had family obligations and could not quit work. He went back to school at night and earned a master's degree in health administration from a local but well-regarded college. This degree plus his ability allowed him to rise to positions of increasing importance in the hospital. At the end of his practitioner period, Jason was managing a large nursing-home facility.

In midlife, Jason decided to cash in his pension and take a doctorate in health administration. He did, landing a tenure-track job. Because Jason had been a manager, he managed his own time well and went up for tenure on schedule. His experience as a practitioner gave him a useful perspective and contacts that contributed to his research and service records.

The Late-Career Childrearing Path

The late-career childrearing path is usually one that women in the past have followed. A woman on this path may have married young, sometimes even before earning an undergraduate degree. Her years as a young married person are devoted to childbearing and rearing and to family matters. If she works, she usually has chosen a job that does not conflict with family functions. At middle age, even if she has a work history she has not yet developed a career path, because a second income is usually the major motive for working outside the home.

In middle age, some women have decided to go to school and earn master's and doctorate degrees. People on this path who remain married may limit their choice of doctoral universities to those within commuting distance. Financially, they use savings, fellowships, and income from their spouses' employment to complete their doctoral studies.

Upon earning Ph.D.s, women on this path seek tenure-earning positions with varying degrees of success. Their success partially depends on their geographic mobility and whether they are in a metropolitan area with greater career opportunities. Those who do land tenure-track jobs then progress toward tenure, often with fewer constraints on their time than younger faculty members trying to juggle competing career and family obligations.

Cathy pursued the late-career childrearing path to tenure. She dropped out of undergraduate school to marry young, and she soon had two children. Her husband ran a major government facility. Cathy worked at the facility in public relations and gained experience working with the press. When she was in her late 30s and her children were older, she decided to return to school to finish her undergraduate degree. She kept on going, and in 10 years completed her doctoral degree.

While Cathy was finishing her degree, her husband died. She was hired on a two-year replacement job at the land-grant college in the same state. Because the position was not permanent, she worked at other universities for three interim years. The land-grant college was anxious to have her return, and when a full-time tenure-track position opened up, department members there made sure she knew about it in advance and applied. Cathy got the job. She negotiated to have all her previous years of teaching count toward tenure, which she earned the next year.

No Single Correct Path

There is no single correct path to tenure. While everyone in theory would like to be a superstar, that path is rare. Most tenure candidates find themselves either consciously or inadvertently following another path. More important for faculty members who wish to remain academics is not which path was pursued, but whether tenure was finally earned. This book has explored strategies to aid in that accomplishment.

Revoking Tenure

Even when earned, tenure still can be lost for one or more reasons. The most common are academic fraud, morals, and finances.

The exact prevalence of fraud within the academy is not known. Evidence is anecdotal. Yet various examples stand out of professors who have had tenure revoked for falsifying their vitae, for falsely claiming publications that do not exist or that were authored by others, and for falsifying research results. People eventually accused of fraud are likely to have moved one or more times; their new institution usually knows about their former achievements mostly from their vitae. The university hiring a professor who has committed fraud takes the candidate's vita at face value. Only later do discrepancies force the school to dig into his or her past to reveal false claims. When fraud is discovered, it is grounds for revoking tenure and dismissing the faculty member in question.

Some professors who have earned tenure lose it for moral reasons. The most common moral reason is sexual harassment and abuse of power over students. Often rumors about such professors have circulated for some time before a formal charge is lodged and an investigation ensues. If the outcome of the investigation determines misconduct, the professor may be forced to resign.

Although it is rare, tenure can be revoked because of an institution's financial troubles, which may force it to lay off tenured faculty members. Sometimes, downsizing may result in entire departments or programs being abolished.

9 | The Ten Commandments of Tenure Success

Tenure is an important milestone in the career of any professor. Like any important milestone, the tenure decision may be approached with dread or with positive determination. Positive determination is the more productivity-enhancing approach, but in either event, the tenure decision is inevitable for faculty who want academic careers. Only in the rarest exceptions of hiring late-in-life distinguished luminaries known for contributions outside of academics can the tenure-review process be personally avoided. Most universities and colleges will not grant tenure without a formal review unless the newly hired professor has already been through a tenure-review process at an equivalent institution within higher education. The tenure-review process then cannot be circumvented. It must be passed successfully to remain a faculty member.

Until you complete this review, we suggest the following as the Ten Commandments of tenure success. Like those from the Old Testament, these are meant to guide daily living. Following all 10 does not guarantee success, but it will enhance the probability of success immensely. These commandments

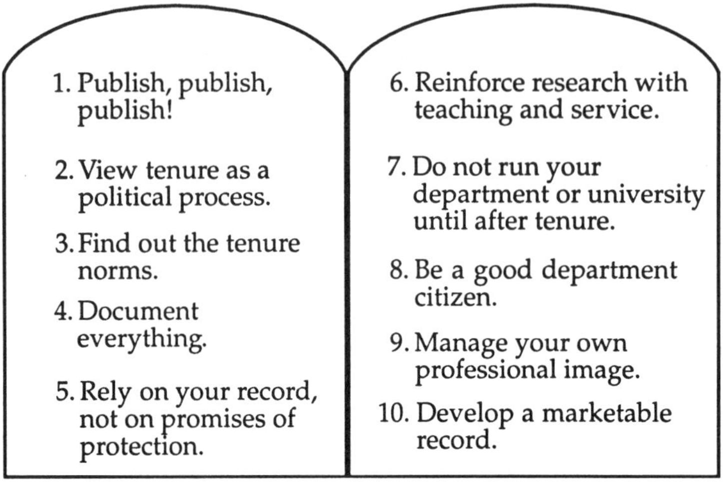

Figure 9.1. The Ten Commandments of Tenure

summarize many of the more important points made throughout this book. (See Figure 9.1.)

❶ *Publish, publish, publish!* The first commandment of tenure success is to publish. Create a personal research agenda and pursue it vigorously. Despite the renewed attention to teaching, most universities and colleges have not abated or reduced their expectations for publications and research. Publish in a peer-reviewed format whenever possible, because it is more highly valued in more places and is indeed a requisite for tenure in most.

At least one third and likely much more of your time in the pretenure period should be devoted to publishing. Do not let other activities crowd out research. Always have one or more articles out for review. Rejections in the peer-review process are inevitable. When an article is rejected at one journal, promptly revise it and send it to another; there usually is a journal home somewhere for most articles. Publish articles instead of books before tenure, unless your field is not scientific and values books more. Collaborate when possible to get more done faster and better, but pick your collaborators carefully.

❷ *View tenure as a political process.* The tenure process is more analogous to a politically charged legislative process than a bureaucratic one. It uses merit as a promotion criterion like a bureaucratic process, although it resembles legislative interactions in several crucial ways. First, peer review is an essential part of departmental decision making and is manifested in some form of majority rule. Second, like legislative criteria for passing bills, the standards for meeting tenure criteria evolve, shift, and are sometimes vague. While outcomes on the extremes may be foregone conclusions, most tenure cases occur within a wide range of potentially acceptable records where political skill is a key factor in the outcome. Third, a tenure candidate must build coalitions for his own case, just as legislators must build coalitions to pass bills. View the tenure process as a legislative one and manage your tenure case much as a floor manager for a bill shepherds it around legislative roadblocks and hurdles.

❸ *Take personal responsibility for finding out the tenure norms.* All universities and colleges use the three criteria of research, teaching, and service to evaluate candidates for tenure. What standards are applied to those three criteria, however, varies widely across institutions and across academic disciplines. In the area of research, for example, more scientific fields value peer-reviewed journal articles and grants. In some fields within the humanities, such as history, a university press book may be expected to meet the research criterion. The number of publications considered adequate, as well as which journals are acceptable and in which ones tenure candidates are expected to publish, also vary across departments and colleges. Departments also differ in their expectations for tenure candidate performance on the teaching and service criteria.

Although tenure criteria are written down for prospective tenure candidates to peruse, the operational standards required to meet the criteria are not. Faculty handbook language may refer to requiring a certain level of performance in qualitative terms, such as "excellent" or "very good," but these qualitative terms do not provide specific information to the tenure candidate. Rather, you must seek out this information informally through discussions with the department chair, senior department members, your dean, and other faculty members who have recently gone through the tenure-review process. The formal tenure packets of recent successful candidates should be examined whenever possible to provide examples of both the substantive content of and format for successful cases.

❹ *Document everything.* As a tenure candidate, you are responsible for submitting the documentation to support your tenure file. This documentation must demonstrate how you have met the major criteria. In some but not all instances, departments may keep teaching evaluations. But normally, tenure candidates must themselves collect and organize information that pertains to their own tenure case. Junior faculty members should never throw anything away that is connected to their job performance. This includes not only teaching evaluations, but also letters from students about teaching, course syllabi, documents showing participation in service activities, copies of requests to review articles and books, letters commending service activities, publications, and conference papers.

Maintaining an updated vita is crucial, and is a task now made much easier by modern word processors. As soon as a new activity will "add a line" to a tenure candidate's curriculum vita, take the time to do so before you forget. Also keep copies of annual performance and activity reports, as well as the written evaluations of chairs and deans. Good record keeping is important to preparing a thorough and well-documented tenure packet.

❺ *Do not rely on your chair or other administrators to protect you from a weak record.* Sometimes prospective tenure candidates are lulled into believing that a department chair or administrator will protect the candidate from deficiencies in his or her record, if the candidate will only perform some time-consuming service or task that the chair or administrator needs done. Do not be lured into this trap. The best defense against a weak record is to not have one! Spend your pretenure decision time wisely, filling in gaps in your record and making up deficiencies, especially those in research.

Promises from department chairs and others to protect a junior faculty member at tenure time should be viewed with suspicion for several reasons. First, the chair may be well intentioned, but given the peer-reviewed nature of the tenure decision and its length with many decision points, no one person can control it. At times, the input from a single decision maker may be crucial, but you cannot tell beforehand if the person trying to persuade you to do something has and will use that kind of clout. Second, administrators change with some frequency, especially in large universities. The chair or dean who promised to protect you may not be in the same position or even at the same institution in two or three years when you need to collect on the promise. Third, not all administrators have your interest at heart. They may be most concerned about pressures bearing on them at the moment, and they may promise things they cannot deliver to resolve their immediate dilemma.

Although it may be tempting to think that you can avoid meeting one of the tenure criteria—say, the research criterion—or get by with lower levels of productivity because some administrator promises to look out for you in the future, only those who still believe in the Tooth Fairy, Santa Claus, and the Easter Bunny should believe such promises. Administrators who really wish to help you will discuss the criteria vis-à-vis your record and help you develop strategies for overcoming deficiencies while there is still time.

❻ *Make teaching and service reinforce research activities.* More tenure candidates have nightmares about meeting the research criterion than the teaching and service criteria. Three main reasons exist for this greater fear of failure. First, absence of productivity is readily apparent. Second, research is among the least structured tenure activity—the one where procrastination is most likely. Third, some departments are finicky not just about the number of publications, but also about the quality of journals in which the tenure candidate's research appears.

One strategy for using time wisely to meet the research criterion is to try to organize teaching and service to reinforce research activities. A supportive department chair will try to give junior faculty members courses to teach in their research areas. In the process of preparing for class, the prospective tenure candidate is collecting articles and information, especially when teaching graduate seminars that are background literature for research projects. While teaching and discussing ideas with students, you may also gain insight that is useful for research and get research ideas.

Sometimes students in advanced and graduate classes can participate in research projects if the course subject is relevant. Co-opting students into research as part of their learning is particularly possible in methodology courses where students are learning research techniques. Similarly, seek out service activities related to your research agenda whenever possible. Integrated research, teaching, and service activities become complementary and even synergistic, reinforcing one another and helping you build a tenurable record.

❼ *Do not try to run the university or your department until you have tenure.* Sometimes junior faculty members get involved in administrative tasks and activities such as serving on the faculty senate, convinced that the university or college would fall apart without their input into discussions and debates. Such junior members get a "rush" from being important and close to decision makers. They drop names of people with whom they have had recent contact or even lunch, such as the college provost, president, and important alumni.

A few very bright and lucky tenure candidates have the skill and energy to run their departments and universities at the same time as they run their own careers and classes. But most do not. Most tenure candidates are better advised to go to the computer center, the library, or advisory meetings with students than to yet another meeting to set university policy. You may be convinced the college cannot make some pending decision without your wisdom and talents, but if you fail to get tenure from neglecting your own research and teaching, then rest assured it will struggle on. Besides, there are administrators who get paid full-time to worry about institutional policies and concerns.

Your first priority should be to your own research and teaching, preferably performing service activities that are related to your own unique expertise. For those tenure candidates with ambitions of a career in university administration, much time remains after the tenure is approved to run the department, college, and university.

❽ *Be a good department citizen.* Although you do not want to be diverted from your own research and teaching, it is important to both project an image of *and* actually be a good department citizen. Certain tasks must be performed to make a department run smoothly and effectively—such as being available during drop-add period to assist students, advising students about courses for the next semester, examining curriculum needs, and so on. Chip in and do your share of these tasks. Shirking these tasks will quickly earn you a reputation as an unsupportive and self-centered colleague, an image that tenure candidates who want their fellow department members to see them as long-term colleagues can ill afford.

Sometimes, little things that do not take much time and effort can enhance your image as a good department citizen: pointing out articles in journals that your colleagues may have missed that are relevant to their research interests, bringing in clippings with the same focus, being willing to guest lecture for colleagues who are sick or must be out of town. Whenever possible, small actions of this type cost little and may be remembered at tenure time. But equally important, they are professionally decent and make work fun.

❾ *Manage your professional image.* A good image that is not backed by a good performance record is a sham that can always be revealed as such at an inopportune time. But a good performance record that is not perceived as such may also produce difficulties at tenure time. The trick, then, is not only to do good work, but also to be perceived as doing so.

Most tenure candidates do not need to hire a Madison Avenue public relations firm to achieve this objective. Rather, judicious conversations with colleagues, apprising colleagues of successes that genuinely give you joy, and self-deprecating humor over failures or faux pas in most cases will be enough. Image management is an important part of the tenure process, just as it is in most occupations and avenues of life, but it is no substitute for productivity.

❿ *Develop a marketable record.* Whenever possible, strive to develop a performance record that is tenurable *anywhere*, not just at your current institution. Sometimes the best laid plans of mice, men, and junior faculty members go awry. In some instances, through no fault of your own, long-term employment in the institution where you originally hoped to get tenure may become undesirable or even impossible. The department may veer off into a direction you find incompatible with your research agenda and teaching interests. Financial exigencies may eliminate tenure-track positions or even whole departments. Increasingly, in dual-career couples with both spouses academics, one spouse may get an offer he or she cannot refuse and the other spouse may decide to follow, seeking a new job in a new location for personal rather than professional reasons.

The best strategy, then, is to develop a record of professional productivity that would be appreciated and tenurable at a wide array of institutions, not just your own current institution. Even if you do not decide to move, the fact that you can develop such a record creates options and prevents the claustrophobic feeling of being trapped. Departments and colleges usually treat faculty members who are productive and potentially mobile better than it does those who are neither. Oh, yes, one last comment about getting tenure: *Good luck!*

Additional Readings

Blackburn, R. T. (1972). *Tenure: Aspects of job security on the changing campus.* Atlanta, GA: Southern Regional Education Board.

Boice, R. (1992). *The new faculty member: Supporting and fostering professional development.* San Francisco: Jossey-Bass.

Bowen, H. R., & Schuster, J. H. (1986). *American professors: A national resource imperiled.* New York: Oxford University Press.

Braskamp, L. A., Brandenburg, D. C., & Ory, J. C. (1984). *Evaluating teaching effectiveness: A practical guide.* Beverly Hills: Sage.

Cahn, S. M. (Ed.). (1978). *Scholars who teach: The art of college teaching.* Chicago: Nelson-Hall.

Centra, J. A. (1979). *Determining faculty effectiveness.* San Francisco: Jossey-Bass.

Clark, S. M., & Lewis, D. R. (Eds.). (1985). *Faculty vitality and institutional productivity: Critical perspectives for higher education.* New York: Teachers College Press.

Commission on Academic Tenure in Higher Education. (1973). *Faculty tenure.* San Francisco: Jossey-Bass.

Ellner, C. L., & Barnes, C. P. (Eds.). (1983). *Studies of college teaching.* Lexington, MA: D. C. Heath.

McKeachie, W. J. (1986). *Teaching tips: A guidebook for the beginning college teacher* (8th ed.). Lexington, MA: D. C. Heath.

Neusner, J. (1984). *How to grade your professors and other unexpected advice.*

Pollard, L. A. (1977). *Women on college and university faculties: A historical survey and a study of their present academic status.* New York: Arno.

Smith, B. L. (Ed.). (1973). *The tenure debate.* San Francisco: Jossey-Bass.

Solomon, R., & Solomon, J. (1993). *Up the university: Re-creating higher education in America.* Reading, MA: Addison-Wesley.

Spencer, M. L., Kehoe. M., & Speece, K. (Eds.). (1982). *Handbook for women scholars: Strategies for success.* San Francisco: Center for Women Scholars, American Behavioral Research Corporation.

Weimer, M. (1990). *Improving college teaching: Strategies for developing instructional effectiveness.* San Francisco: Jossey-Bass.

Also of interest:

Benjaminson, P. (1992). *Publish without perishing: A practical handbook for academic authors.* Washington, DC: NEA Professional Library.

Day, R. (1981). *How to write and publish a scientific paper.* Philadelphia: Institute for Scientific Information.

Fox, M. F. (Ed.). (1985). *Scholarly writing and publishing.* Boulder, CO: Westview.

Geiser, E., Dolen, A., & Topkis, G. (Eds.). (1985). *The business of book publishing.* Boulder, CO: Westview.

Horning, L. S. (1979). *Climbing the academic ladder.* Washington, DC: National Academy of Sciences.

Horowitz, I. L. (1991). *Communicating ideas: The politics of scholarly publishing* (2nd ed.). New Brunswick, NJ: Transaction Books.

Matkin, R. E., & Riggar, T. F. (Eds.). (1991). *Persist and publish: Helpful hints for academic writing and publishing.* Niwot: University Press of Colorado.

Moxley, J. M. (1992). *Publish, don't perish: the scholar's guide to academic writing and publishing.* Westport, CT: Greenwood.

Mullins, C. J. (1977). *A guide to writing and publishing in the social and behavioral sciences.* New York: John Wiley.

Schoenfeld, C. (1992). *Mentor in a manual: Climbing the academic ladder to tenure.* Madison, WI: Magna.

Seldin, P. (1991). *The teaching portfolio: A practical guide to improved performance and promotion/tenure decisions.* Bolton, MA: Anker.

Van Till, W. (1981). *Writing for professional publications.* Boston: Allyn & Bacon.

For details about tenure regulations, contact the American Association of University Professors, 1012 14th Street, Suite 500, Washington, DC 20005; (202) 737-5900.

About the Authors

Marcia Lynn Whicker (Ph.D., University of Kentucky, 1976) is Professor of Public Administration at the Graduate School at Rutgers, Newark. Her publications include 12 books, more than 45 peer-reviewed articles, and more than 50 nonpeer-reviewed and journalistic articles in the areas of public policy, public administration, and U.S. politics. Her interests include using computer-simulation models to test the effectiveness and representativeness of governmental structures and systems.

Jennie Jacobs Kronenfeld (Ph.D., Brown University, 1976) is Professor of Health Administration in the College of Business at Arizona State University in Tempe. She has published 5 books and 100 articles in the areas of health services research, health administration, health education, health policy, and women and health. She also has specialized in survey research on health issues.

Ruth Ann Strickland (Ph.D., University of South Carolina, 1989) is Associate Professor of Political Science and Criminal Justice at Appalachian State University in Boone, North Carolina. She has published a book on constitutional change and numerous articles in the areas of U.S. politics, public policy, criminal justice, and legal process. Her research approaches have ranged from traditional survey research to multivariate aggregate data models and computer simulations.